SMALL BRAND AMERICA

A look at 25 tiny U.S. brands succeeding in a world dominated by giant competitors

BY
STEVE AKLEY

Written and Published by:
Steve Akley

To Amy:

My beautiful wife and partner in everything!

Preface

"I have been up against tough competition all of my life. I wouldn't know how to get along without it."
    - Walt Disney

Grocery stores have always fascinated me. It's the place where you seek out all of the brands you hear so much about on TV, radio and billboards. The grocery store is home to the Smuckers® family, The Three Musketeers™, Mrs. Butterworth™, Toucan Sam™ and many more. It's also a battlefield where companies go to war over consumer interest and shelf space. Marketing is often being conducted right there directly to the consumer (shelf hangers, displays, shelf placement, samples, etc.).

I was so intrigued with the activities and products of a grocery store, I spent the first part of my career working in the industry. I started at the age of sixteen working for a local chain in my hometown of St. Louis. I continued to work there all through high school, college and a few years after.

If you spend enough time working at a store, at some point, you end up working every job in the store. My experience was no exception. I started out bagging groceries and wrangling shopping carts. I transitioned to stocking shelves and occasionally checking. When individuals took vacations, I would often serve in other roles in the meat, dairy or produce departments. In college I actually worked as the overnight manager of a 24-hour store. It often alternated between boredom, fright and hilarity working those overnight shifts! That literally could easily be another book by itself. The end result, though, is you learning the business. You see how the products are sold to consumers at the store.

About a year or so after I graduated from college, I went to work for a food broker. Unlike being in a store where it is strictly a retail environment, working for the broker opened me up to the wholesale side of the business.

Food brokers represent companies which do not want to employ a sales force to bring their products to market. They pay a percentage of the price of their goods to a company to sell their products and represent it in a given marketplace. As such, not only are you given sales quotas, but also you have to work with local chains to promote the products. You are responsible for new item rollouts (getting them on the shelf) as well as protecting the coveted space you secured once you had successfully gotten the product on the shelf. The grocery business is all about shelf space. Where your item is located in terms of height, placement in a section, and what it is next to, can really have a major impact on how well it sells.

While I represented some of the most well-known brands in America during my time with the food broker, I also really got a sense of what it is like for the smaller brands. It was always interesting to see how those companies who didn't have the multi-million dollar budgets, their own sales force, or perhaps not even food-broker representation would try to compete with the much larger brands I was representing. It literally would not be uncommon to run into the owner of a small regional brand pitching his or her product to a store owner while trying to get the item "cut" onto the store shelf ("cut" being an industry term meaning something else has to be removed or reduced to get a new item worked in).

In many cases, these smaller brands may have had a product which was far superior to the better known "national" brands. For the megabrands, quality is often sacrificed when you are trying to squeeze every penny of profit out of products so corners are cut on ingredients to be as profitable as possible for the shareholders of their publicly held companies.

It's different for small companies. Their economies of scale mean that right out of the gate they are going to be more expensive than a nationally known brand, and they aren't going to be able to generate the buzz of an ad on a top-rated TV show or sporting event. Still, through a variety of means, they compete.

Whether it's by out hustling, offering a better product, the benefit of not have the expenses the major brands incur, or perhaps a combination of all of the above, each category dominated by 2 or 3 large national brands, often has 25 or more small brands trying to fight their way onto those same shelves.

One might wonder if it is even worth showcasing some of these small brands. After all, the megabrands are happy to gobble up as much shelf space as a retailer will allow them. A constant influx of new items, combined with a desire to garner more real estate for their flagship brands, means the biggest players are trying to come up with creative ways to squeeze the little guys out.

The truth of the matter is the public, the grocers and even the megabrands need these companies.

For the consumer, it's all about choices and ensuring quality standards are maintained as market share goes up for the big companies.

The grocers want these small brands to offer a variety of products, price points and to introduce a local flair to their store.

While the big brands might tell you they do not need small brands trying to take "their" space, the truth is they do. Keeping them in check via the quality and price competition of the small brands, means that fair trade is maintained for the consumer. In the end, they have better products and are kept in check in terms of price which translates into satisfactory consumer experiences. In-turn, satisfied customers mean consumers continue to buy the megabrands' products even when there are other competitors on the shelves.

The goal of **Small Brand America** is to introduce 25 companies competing in a world dominated by megabrands. Each company will be listed by segment (like "hot sauce, mustard or honey") and profiled with company information, a look at their products and company history as well as the stories of the individuals who run these organizations.

Noted retailer Marshall Field once said, "*Goodwill is the only asset that competition cannot undersell or destroy.*"

Keeping Mr. Field's comment in mind, I'm pleased to introduce these 25 brands to you. Hopefully, the next time you are in the grocery store and you happen to see one of these products sitting on the bottom shelf with the megabrands sitting at eye-level, you will pause and take a second look at them. Remembering their ideals, the hard work which goes into competing against much larger competitors and the stories of those individuals who drive these organizations, you may decide to drop one of these products in your basket.

After all, each one represents **Small Brand America**!

Table of Contents

Chapter 1: Bacon

Des Moines Bacon Company

412 South 8th Street
Adel, IA
(515) 664-3141

desmoinesbaconcompany.com
info@desmoinesbaconcompany.com

Established
2011

Leadership
Jim & Rachel Reis, Owners

Products
Maple Cured Bacon, Smoked Chipotle Bacon, Italian Herb Bacon and Hardwood Smoked Uncured Bacon

Until you've experienced dry curing, you haven't really had bacon...

In 2009, fed up with bacon which shrunk down to a shell of itself and tasted like salted smoke, Jim Reis decided to try his hand at making his own bacon in his backyard. After all, he had smoked his own briskets and pork for pulled-pork for years. How hard could it be?

He participated in a seminar to learn exactly how preparing your own bacon worked. He then bought a pork belly, seasoned it, smoked it and, sure enough, it was way better than anything he had ever found at the supermarket. He had found bacon nirvana!

The best part was when he cooked up a slice of bacon, he actually had a slice of bacon, not something that looked like a shriveled piece of flattened meat. As he shared it with friends, he knew he was onto something special because they would just rave about what he was making versus what they had been conditioned to think bacon was by the large meat companies who paid millions to advertise and promote their version of bacon (or perhaps better stated, "bacon").

Jim began to experiment with different seasonings and approaches to smoking his pork bellies. Before long, he was confident he had a product which could find an audience on store shelves.

The key to his process is the dry curing. Jim seasons his pork bellies and then lets them sit refrigerated for a week. This is the curing phase of his process, and it is the time when those flavors begin to marry. Once the curing is complete, he then smokes them to seal in the flavor.

The main difference between his process and the large well-known name brands happens at the curing phase. Corners are cut in curing by injecting flavoring into the pork belly. This initiates several key components to stretch profits. First of all, the curing process is shortened. You do not have to blend spice and meat together and wait a week for that flavoring to absorb.

Secondly, injecting soluble solutions into the meat means that a pound of bacon isn't a pound of meat. That's why their bacon shrinks up so much during cooking. It's not just the fat rendering down; it's also those water-based solutions cooking out.

The final reason these companies take this shortcut is the shortened time needed to smoke the product. Their flavoring is sealed in via the injections so it lessens the time needed on the smoker.

All of this adds up to more profits, but it is clearly and inferior product for the consumer. Jim Reis set out with a plan to introduce a new kind of bacon to consumers: one that doesn't cut corners and delivers a quality product.

In 2011, with his recipes set and a business plan in place, he proceeded to the State of Iowa. Admittedly, he knew this plan was small. He was going to do this without outside investors so he was looking at a very small, hands-on operation.

When he presented his plan to the individuals he would need to approve his venture, he was told steadfastly it could not be done. Because of the inherent dangers in dealing with raw meat, it must be processed in either a state or federal approved meat processing plant.

He was told the numbers he brought to them as a start-up company were just too insignificant. He was looking at processing about 250 lbs. at a time. There wouldn't be a meat locker (where meat must be processed) which could work on such a small scale. To find a meat locker interested in working with him, he was told the minimum run would need to be in the range of 1,500 – 2,000 lbs.

That could be the end of the story, but Jim wasn't going to let this hiccup stop him. He personally began to call each meat locker in Iowa. Didn't matter where: *have meat will travel* was his mantra!

After many phone calls, he found a small town, not too far away (about 40 miles), which was willing to work with him within the parameters he needed. With that, the Des Moines Bacon Company was officially born!

Working with this meat locker meant Jim still was able to mix his own spices to flavor the bacon. Per the state guidelines, spices must be applied to the meat, refrigerated, then smoked and packaged onsite.

Initially, he began selling his product at farmer's markets. He very quickly knew he had a winner when he would see the same individuals buying his product each week. Feedback was always incredibly positive with people raving about the taste and quality of his bacon.

With the success of direct sale to consumers via farmer's markets, Jim began to explore the idea of actually getting his product on store shelves. A farmer by trade, he didn't have any experience working in the grocery industry so his approach was simply to jump in and ask the meat manager about carrying his product.

He was surprised to find dealing directly with the meat managers was a very pleasant experience. They liked the idea of offering a higher quality product and were also in-tune with offering a local product to their customers.

Being the person who owns the company, sells the product and delivers it has been an easy way for Jim to build rapport with the meat managers. These relationships mean his product has received very favorable shelf placement. In-turn, this has translated into strong sales.

Of course, running a small company by yourself has its challenges. Jim, along with his uncle, have continued to farm soybeans. Spring (planting) and fall (harvesting) are so busy that Jim has pulled his dad out of retirement to help with store maintenance. A typical week (during the farm's non-peak times) looks like this for him:

Monday – Visit the stores where he has product placement. See how his bacon sold over the weekend (the busiest time for grocery stores) and replenish stock where needed.

Tuesday – Mix cures. Buy pork bellies and take them, along with the mixed cures, to the meat locker for processing.

Wednesday – Work on the farm.

Thursday – Pick up processed bacon and begin delivering products to stores to stock-up for the weekend.

Friday – Complete delivery of bacon to the balance of the grocery stores/specialty stores that carry Des Moines Bacon.

Saturday – Sell product direct at the farmer's market.

Sunday – Sell product direct at the farmer's market.

In between, Jim is married to his wife Rachel, and they have a two-year-old son. Needless to say, he is incredibly busy and there is plenty of sacrifices made by the entire family.

Along with all of the hard work, there are rewards as well. In 2013, the Des Moines Bacon Company participated in the Bacon Festival held at the Iowa State Fairgrounds. This isn't just a bunch of weekend warriors showing off their backyard cooking skills. It is serious competition where every major player who sells bacon is represented.

Sound like something you might be interested in?

They sold 8,500 tickets to the event this year. It sold out in four (not a typo--4) minutes!

As you can imagine it is a bacon-frenzy, and the stakes are high to succeed. Every competitor is treated exactly the same. Whether you are doing 250 lbs. runs (like Jim) or you typically sell 250 lbs. of bacon every .5 second (megabrands), your product is on an even keel.

The Des Moines Bacon Company garnered two awards at the event. They were the Best Dry Cured Bacon winner and the Grand Champion which recognizes the best overall bacon. In the bacon world, that's like one team winning the Super Bowl and the World Series in the same year!

Jim Reis is about to take the Des Moines Bacon Company on a whole new journey. From its very humble beginnings, the company is already at the capacity of the small town meat locker he was once told he would never find. The next step means that Jim will need to move to a federally inspected facility which will allow him to sell his bacon to grocery stores around the country.

To sell nationally, there is a lot of paperwork and legwork which he needs to do to get the approvals needed through Washington, DC. He's up for the task though. Doing so will ease up a bit on the hands-on work he is doing now as his one-man show.

In terms of new products, there may be a habanero bacon on the horizon. He realizes this is a niche market product, but he's been working with flavoring and has a blend he believes would be appealing. Getting package approval for a new product can be just as daunting as creating it, however. All labeling for food must be federally approved, and this is a process that can take a small company like Des Moines Bacon up to 8 or 9 months for final approval.

Jim envisions the company branching out from just bacon, as well. He is getting close to introducing a smoked ham to his product mix. Long term, he sees specialty sausages, pancetta and prosciutto in the product line, too.

With the love affair America has with bacon, it is a great time to be in the business. Websites, t-shirts and fanatics all laud the appeal of bacon. Jim knows this is a fad, but the love for a good quality product will always be there. He has positioned himself well to succeed for the long term.

The Des Moines Bacon Company Photo Album

Des Moines Bacon Company Owner Jim Reis

Team Des Moines Bacon Company

Serving up bacon at the farmer's market

Some of Jim Reis' prized Heritage breed pigs

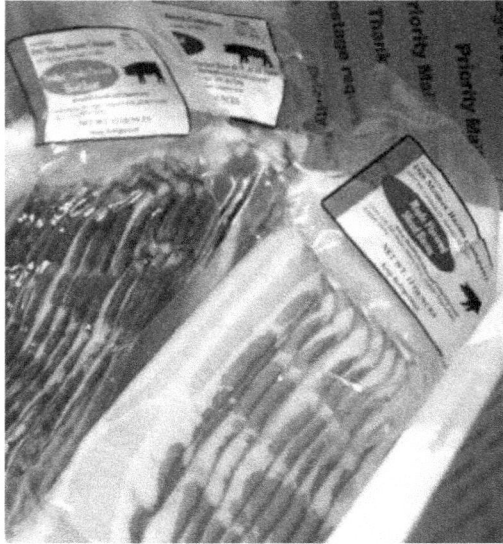

Packaged bacon

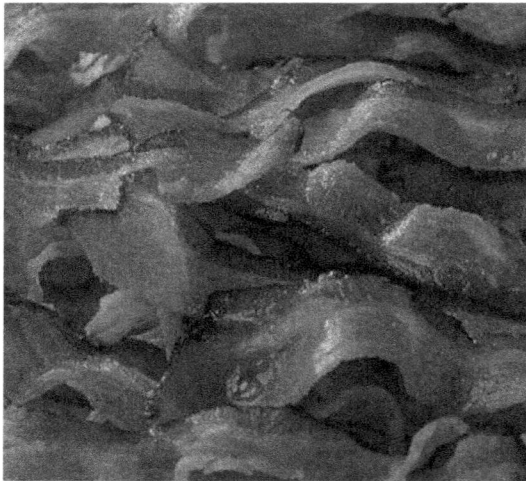

The final product

Chapter 2: Beer

Alaskan Brewing Company

ALASKAN BREWING CO. ®

5429 Shaune Drive
Juneau, AK 99801
(907) 780-5866

alaskanbeer.com
info@alaskanbeer.com

Established
1986

Leadership
Marcy & Geoff Larson, Co-Owners

Products
Alaskan Amber, Alaskan Freeride APA, Alaskan IPA, Alaskan White, Alaskan Stout, Spring/Summer/Winter Seasonal Beers as well as various limited edition offerings

The great American import…

Starting a new beer company today might not be very newsworthy. After all, according to 2013 Brewer's Associations statistics, there more than 2,400 breweries spread out across the United States as our country continues to experience its second "brewery boom."

Before Prohibition, America's thirst for beer was quenched by more than 2,500 breweries. These ranged from large scale national brewers, many of which are still in business today, to small scale operations which would now be defined as micro or craft brewers.

Not being able to manufacture or sell their products during Prohibition had an obvious negative impact on the breweries, and the numbers thinned quickly. At the low point, the U.S. had approximately 25 brewers.

After Prohibition, with few competitors left on the landscape and a consumer who was about to be introduced to new forms of advertising via television, the stage was set for an era of "beer wars" where the megabrands would fight for consumer loyalty.

Changes to legislature in the 1980's made it easier for a company to get into brewing, but consumer tastes were now linked to the megabrands whom they had grown to embrace.

America was about to experience a renaissance in beer, but in 1986, when Marcy and Geoff Larson were exploring the idea of opening a brewery, it was a unproven proposition. At the time, there were only 66 other brewers in the United States. They weren't looking at just any location either. They were exploring the idea of opening a brewery in Juneau, Alaska, a town only accessible by sea plane or boat as it is bordered by the Pacific waters of the Inside Passage and the Tongass National Forest.

Even with the knowledge that the Alaskan Brewing Company is a success today, when you take yourself back to the time when they got started and understand the conditions in which they began this journey, you might question how they were able to survive and ultimately thrive. Then again, to question the success, you obviously don't know Marcy and Geoff Larson.

The couple met while working in Glacier National Park in Montana. They had a shared love of the outdoors and spirit of adventure. Their dream of working in the ultimate outdoor adventure, Alaska, was fulfilled when Marcy got a job at Glacier Bay National Park. Geoff would soon follow her to Alaska.

When their time at Glacier Bay was over, Marcy and Geoff weren't ready to leave Alaska. They got other jobs, but those positions too ended. They moved to Juneau with a goal of finding a way to make a living.

A friend suggested opening a brewery. It made sense since Geoff was home brewing already, and he had always received a strong positive feedback for his beer.

Marcy began to research the history of brewing in Alaska. During the Alaskan Gold Rush of the late 1890's – early 1900's, there had been several small brewers catering specifically to the mining towns.

Of particular interest was one known as the Douglas Brewing Company. The brewer was in business from 1899 – 1907 on a small island about a ½ mile across from Juneau (it is now considered part of Juneau but was separate at the time). In her research, she uncovered information about a particularly well-liked beer from the company. Her research also included a partial ingredient list for Douglas Brewing Company's most popular offering.

Geoff decided to take a shot at brewing this beer himself. He had to take a few liberties to round out the recipe list, but he did so utilizing what would be available to a late 19th century/early 20th century brewer. He, along with anyone to whom he provided a sample, was amazed at how great this product tasted. Ultimately, Geoff's creation would become Alaskan Amber, Alaskan Brewing Company's flagship beer, but they still had plenty of work ahead to get this venture off the ground.

With a business plan in place, a legal landscape open to starting a new brewery and a recipe to start with, Marcy and Geoff headed to the bank to secure funding. Despite passion, solid business plan, and great product, the banks simply weren't willing to offer funding for a brewery in a state with no agriculture and more than 1,000 miles by boat to Seattle. The banks said the area was too remote, it was too expensive to get ingredients there and a brewery was too risky in-general.

Undeterred, Geoff and Marcy sought investors. Literally going door-to-door in Juneau and around Alaska with a business plan in hand, they met with individuals about investing in their Alaskan Brewing Company. Finally, with 88 investors in place, in December of 1986, the Alaskan Brewing Company became the 67th brewer in the United States.

With very little equipment, they began with a hands-on process of preparing and packaging their beer. Their first order, 253 cases, took Marcy, Geoff and ten volunteers twelve hours to hand package. Early profits were invested back into the company so they could get up-and-running to meet demand.

In 1987, their first full year in business, Geoff and Marcy began attending the Great American Beer Festival (GABF) in Denver, Colorado. While much smaller at the time, today, GABF is the premier beer festival for breweries to compare and contrast their products versus that of their competitors as more than 3,000 beers are judged in 120 different categories. Gold, Silver and Bronze *may be awarded* for each category. Alaskan Brewing Company is the most awarded craft brewer in the history of this festival, and their Smoked Porter is the most recognized beer with over 23 medals.

Currently, the company offers the following five beers:

Alaskan Amber - Their flagship beer is based on a turn-of-the-century recipe that quenched the thirst of miners during the Klondike Gold Rush. Smooth and richly malty, this altbier goes well with any meal.

Alaskan Freeride APA - Alaskan Freeride APA features a lush, green, almost tropical hop aroma paired with the unique taste combination of these three, distinctive hop varieties, making it both full in flavor and crisply thirst-quenching.

Alaskan IPA - The very intense, complex aromatic character with a refreshing, crisp finish is achieved by dry hopping. The fruity, citrusy aroma is a nice complement with grilled prawns and spicy foods.

Alaskan White - The unique aroma of coriander and the crisp finish of orange peel of this witbier pairs well with spicy foods and lighter fare such as seafood and salads.

Alaskan Stout - This beer offers the richness of stouts without the harshness. It pairs well with hearty meals, chocolate and desserts. It also makes a delightful fireside sipper.

In addition to their year round beers, they also offer seasonal Spring, Summer and Winter brews. The company also features several series of limited edition beers. These are brewed in small quantities and available for short periods.

The first limited edition is their award-winning Smoked Porter. This dark and robust beer is created each November 1 features a smoky flavor and a process that ages the beer in the bottle like a fine wine.

Their Pilot Series are small batch releases of brewing styles and flavors which showcase the creativity of the company and its brewers. The best of their "in-house experiments" ultimately end up getting distributed via their Pilot Series.

The final component to Alaskan Brewing Company's limited releases is their "Rough Draft" Series. This unique approach allows anyone in the company to research a brewing idea, team with their fellow employees and create a new offering. Brewing teams might be comprised of individuals from accounting, sales and customer service utilizing Alaskan's 1 or 10 barrel brewing systems. Initially, these beers were only available in Alaska. Recently, the company has begun shipping them to the "lower 48" as well.

Of course, getting beer from Juneau to the 14 western states they currently service is enough of a challenge that they occasionally get called the "Great American Import." Shipping to Seattle, the hub from which their beer gets distributed involves palletizing their beer and loading it in shipping containers. They then deliver the containers to the port in Juneau. Ships leave Juneau most days, though that can vary by season and is based upon weather. It then takes one week to get to Seattle. From there, it is shipped either via truck or rail car depending on the final destination.

Alaskan Brewing Company then has sales representatives, supplemented by distributors who introduce their product to new venues within assigned territories. The company supports their efforts in the field with point-of-sale material and advertising within the markets. A recent promotion entitled the Seattle Gold Rush has gotten them a lot of publicity. A golden ticket, good for a nugget of gold valued at $10,000, was hidden at a secret location in Seattle, and the company has been releasing hints to assist individuals in finding it.

Today, Marcy and Geoff are still actively involved in the company though they have begun to look ahead to retirement. Currently, they are in the process of transitioning out of the business by ultimately converting the company from their ownership to being an organization owned by its employees.

Treating their employees well has always been a driving force behind the success of the company. Marcy and Geoff learned quickly that if your employees are treated well, and empowered to make decisions, you do not have to manage anyone when the right people are in place. They work together to ensure the company is producing the best product possible.

As the 16th largest craft brewer and a history of award-winning beers, it seems Marcy and Geoff have found the perfect formula for success!

Alaskan Brewing Company Photo Album

Geoff and Marcy Larson

Alaskan Brewing Company's award wall

Alaskan Brewing Company's brewing building

Alaskan Amber coming off of the line

A few of the company's beers in their natural environment

Cheers!

Chapter 3: Blue Cheese

Berkshire Cheese, LLC

Berkshire Blue
CHEESE
Made completely by hand of
WHOLE UNPASTEURIZED
Jersey
COWS' MILK
from Berkshire County, Massachusetts   lbs.
by
BERKSHIRE CHEESE, L.L.C.
P.O. Box 35, Dalton, MA 01227
at its
Great Barrington, Mass.,
Dairy Plant 25-115
AND AGED 60 DAYS.
Batch made of milk, salt, starter cultures, blue & white molds and vegetable rennet. This is an all-natural product. Store at 38F, but serve at room temperature.

P.O. Box 35
Dalton, MA 01227
(413) 842-5128

berkshirecheese.com
ira@berkshirecheese.com

Established
1998

Leadership
Ira Grable, Cheese Maker

Products
Artisan blue cheese

Drumming up sales for Blue Cheese...

From 1980 – 2000, Ira Grable's family had a successful domestic and export textile business in New York. As with many small companies, Ira did a little bit of everything: working in sales, quality control, shipping and receiving and management among other responsibilities. When the business was shutdown, Ira began looking for a new opportunity. He thought it might be time to pursue a long time dream of his to become a full-time musician.

He ended up in Dalton, Massachusetts where he tried unsuccessfully to break-in as a studio musician. He found the local music scene to not be as happening as he had initially assessed it to be. When bands did need a studio drummer, his instrument of choice, they ended up using the individuals who were already working in the area.

Out of work, he began searching for opportunities. A conversation with a neighbor led to his big break: not in the music scene but instead in the cheese scene!

His neighbor knew a former newspaper publisher who had started a small cheese company. He was trying to build the business by himself and was in desperate need of help to assist in growing the business. After the two of them spoke, they agreed, that perhaps with Ira's assistance, the business could begin to grow beyond what the owner had been able to do on his own.

Berkshire Blue Cheese began in 1998 after the friend of Ira's neighbor took a vacation to England where he visited a cheese manufacturer who made blue cheese. He convinced the owner of the business to give him samples of the cultures/starters which would allow him to create the same cheese in the United States.

Back in the U.S., he began recreating Berkshire Blue just as he had learned to do in England. With its bold and unique flavor,

Berkshire Blue Cheese was an immediate hit in the local specialty stores and restaurants. People were amazed to discover the taste of a real artisanal blue cheese versus their preconceived idea of a blue cheese formed by years of buying the large consumer brands from the grocery store.

Despite its rave reviews, the company hadn't really grown. It was hamstrung by the fact most of the owner's time had been dedicated to making the cheese, leaving little time to market it beyond the immediate area.

When Ira came aboard, he became a one-man public relations/marketing/sales/distribution team. He was still drumming, but instead of playing percussion, he was drumming up sales for Berkshire Blue!

Ira relished life on the road. He would get on his motorcycle and go out and sell cheese. Often, he would spend 12 – 14 hours a day (or longer) making appointments, cold-calling and delivering product.

The partnership was going great, and they were steadily growing the business. After a period of large-scale growth by start-up standards, Ira began to notice some issues with the quality of the product. There would be batches that were too salty. Others were too pungent. Still others suffered from high acid levels or consistency issues from not having been set properly.

It all made sense one day when Ira's old friend told him he had lost the passion for the business and was going to retire. He had grown tired of the business, and he was going to simply close the doors.

While Ira had made his living on the sales side of the business, and not the cheese-making side, he didn't want to simply let the business go. From his direct contact with customers, he knew the potential of this business.

In 2009, Ira worked out a deal to buy the company with the stipulation his friend would stay onboard for six-months to teach Ira exactly how to make Berkshire Blue Cheese. Ira's purchase was a renaissance for the company. There was once again a dedication and passion for making a consistent product with each-and-every wheel.

Making Berkshire Blue Cheese is a full-time job. It is a labor-intensive process which begins at 4:30 a.m. each day with a visit to a local farm to pick up the supply of milk for the day. One of Ira's early wins was to establish a relationship with a farmer who allowed him the benefit of getting the milk from the same source every day. He personally drives the truck to pick up milk, straight from the cows, from a farm which only sells its product to him.

With the purchase and change in job responsibilities, there was no longer a salesperson on the road driving sales, so he turned to a different source to get his product to consumers: distributors. This calculated move meant he was earning less for each cheese wheel, but the distributors had the proper contacts and the sales channels to reach further than he ever could have on his motorcycle.

With the tentacles of the distribution network reaching further than Berkshire Blue Cheese had before, the company began to once again experience serious growth. Berkshire was also quickly growing far beyond the realm of a regional product with stores as far as California purchasing his cheese.

The ultimate testament to the great work Ira was doing in his role of cheese maker came about when **Bon Appétit**® magazine came calling. Seeing his cheese featured on the front cover of a nationally recognized magazine was a thrill and affirmation that Ira had done the right thing by buying the company and continuing to produce its cheese.

With a growing demand for his product Ira did try a few new product lines. He is somewhat limited to what he can offer in his current location, though. Blue cheese has such a formidable scent so only variations of it can be produced in a given facility. Other types of cheese begin to take on the flavor of the blue cheese as it cures even if they are stored in a different area than the blues.

The first variation Ira tried was a smoked blue cheese. The first year, sales were pretty solid so he tried it again the next year. The second time around it did sell, but not at the level it had previously. He ended up using the remainder of his stock as holiday gifts.

His second offering was a blue cheese salad dressing. Ira's mixture was well-received in terms of flavor. His problem in moving his blue cheese dressing was based on the amounts he was creating, as well as the premium ingredients he used, meant it was priced so far over the national brands he couldn't get people to commit to buying it.

For the time being, Ira is focusing solely on growing his flagship blue business. Today, he is nearing capacity of his 1,100 square foot facility. Future growth means that he is going to have to find a new production plant as well as a different source for milk.

Berkshire continues to expand both at retail and through food service where Ira is seeing more chefs utilizing the unique taste of his cheese in their recipes. The cheese continues to receive global recognition winning awards in London, Dublin, New York, Boston and Italy to name a few.

Despite the success, Ira is committed to keeping to the hand-made approach that has gotten him the success to this point. He works with the farmer he has partnered with to ensure the cows are eating correctly to produce the best milk and ultimately cheese. He keeps to the standards he learned when he took over the company.

The only machinery he utilizes in his process is the truck to get the milk, the pump to get the milk to-and-from the truck, the heater to keep him warm in the winter and a refrigerator for the cheese. The rest is done by hand including the mixing of ingredients, cutting of the curd, separating the whey, turning the curing cheese and packaging the finished product.

Everything seems to be working well. Not only is his cheese in specialty and grocery store, fine restaurants and exclusive hotels, it is also in some high profile venues. Some of these include Yankee Stadium™, Citi Field™ (where the Mets® play), TD Bank Center Arena™ (Boston) and even the United Nations.

Not too bad for an out-of-work studio drummer!

Berkshire Cheese Photo Album

Ira Grable

Ira at work

Quality inspection

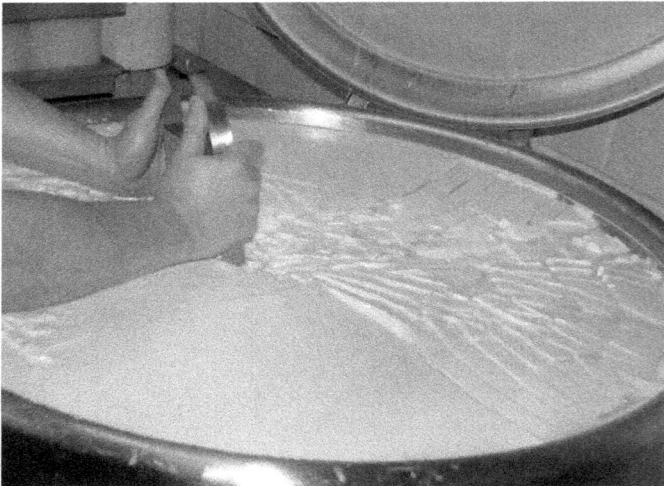

Cutting the cheese curd

Before aging

Blue cheeses in various stages of aging

Cheese wheels with one cut open

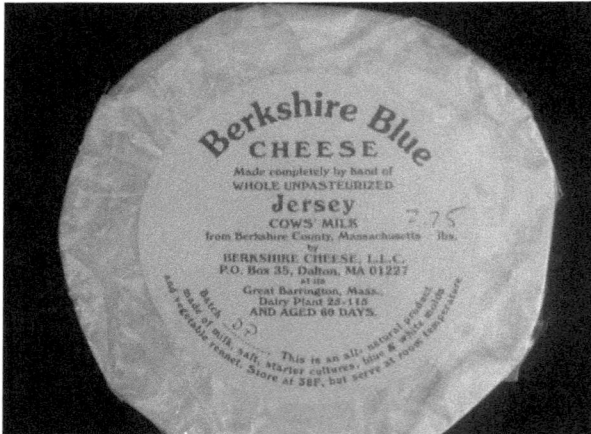

A finished wheel of Berkshire Blue Cheese

Chapter 4: Candy Bars
Idaho Candy Company

412 South 8ᵗʰ Street
Boise, ID 83702
(208) 342-5505
(800) 8-Yum-Yum

idahospud.com
info@idahospud.com

Established
1901

Leadership
David Wagers, Candyman

Products
Idaho Spud Bar (potato-shaped candy bar), Cherry Cordials (milk chocolate and ground peanuts surrounding a whole cherry fondant center) and Old Faithful Peanut Cluster (chocolate peanut cluster with a marshmallow center), Huckleberry Gems (gem-shaped huckleberry-flavored marshmallow crèmes covered in milk chocolate) and Owyhee Butter Toffee (chunk style, bite sized and chocolate covered)

Introducing the Spud Bar…

If you ask 1,000 people to name three things representing Idaho, you would be hard-pressed to find anyone who doesn't mention the potato. With this in mind, it makes perfect sense for an Idaho-based company to produce a candy bar that *looks* like a potato. Today, the Idaho Candy Company churns out approximately 2,000,000 Idaho Spud Bars a year along with a variety of other confections which takes consumers back to yesteryear.

The company started in 1901, in Boise, Idaho, when T.O. Smith, who was a former candy maker and current out-of-work construction worker, decided to go into business for himself. He drew upon his past work in the candy business to start making his own candy and selling it door-to-door out of shoe boxes.

Early success allowed him to open a small shop where he employed seventeen women who would hand-dip his chocolate bars. Business continued to build to the point that a new building was warranted. Mr. Smith took on a partner in the Adams family of Boise and built a modern factory at 412 South 8th Street in Boise in 1909.

This 23,000 square foot facility was state-of-the-art at the time and featured such amenities as sky lights and "welfare" (break rooms) for the employees. Today, the Idaho Candy Company continues to operate in this facility, utilizing much of the same equipment it did in the early 1900's.

The company developed what was to become their most well-known product in 1918 with the invention of the aforementioned Spud Bar. The "potato-looking" bar is made with light cocoa and a soft marshmallow center and drenched in dark chocolate and sprinkled with cocoa. Today, the Spud Bar is a favorite in the Northwest, and Idaho Candy sells them directly to consumers in twelve states in the area.

In 1984, local businessman John Wagers had grown tired of running his own accounting practice. The long hours and pressure had left him feeling burnt out, and he was looking for a change. When someone told him local businessman Don Wakeman, who had purchased the Idaho Candy Company in 1969, was selling out, he was interested. He had no candy-making experience at all, but the thought of making candy for a living sounded fun.

Trading dealing with reports, tax season, deadlines and the mundane aspects of accounting to making candy bars each day appealed to him. In making candy, it was going to be a little bit of Willy Wonka® each and every day.

With that, the candy maker wannabe jumped in. John Wagers purchased the company and began living his dream. You may think someone who doesn't have any experience in making candy would be so out of his element that unforeseen difficulties would overwhelm him.

While John certainly had no knowledge of candy making, he had a committed staff in place, and he had excellent business acumen. One of the benefits of coming from his background in accounting was he met individuals who ran their businesses well and others who did not. The ability to see how top performers manage their company and finances was vital in helping him set a path of success for the Idaho Candy Company.

One of his committed team members was a woman named Violet "Vi" Brewer. She began working at the factory in 1913 at the age of thirteen. Her mother took ill, and she needed to go to work to help support the family. She began shoveling coal in the furnace and eventually moved her way up to hand-dipping chocolates. She held that position for 50 years until she moved to the weighing department where she worked another 30 years. In total, at her retirement, Vi had worked for Idaho Candy 82 years!

Of course if you work for a place for a long time (say 20 years or more), there has to be some good stories, and Vi had a favorite. Around 1919, Vi, then a 19 year-old, was spotted in a dance club, and it was reported to management at the factory.

While laughable now, this was pretty scandalous for a conservative town at that time. Despite the fact she had only gone to dance, and not drink, management decided to let her go. Apparently, the "firing" didn't take, though, because the next day Vi showed up for work and just kept doing her job. No one said anything and coolers heads must have prevailed with management because nobody sent her home. She continued to do this each day and, thankfully, the company kept paying her. After all, this allowed Vi to finish out the last 76 years of her career with Idaho Candy! In retirement, Vi passed at the age of 101, but she was noted to have lived a "sweet life."

John's son Dave started working for the business when his father purchased the company. He left for a while after he graduated college to work for a large technology company. After working a few years outside of the family business, Dave came back and helped out his father. Coming from a traditional business, combined with his work in college, Dave came back as the plant manager and felt he would dress appropriately by wearing the traditional uniform of management: a coat and tie.

When his team of chocolate dippers began to laugh at him, he wondered what was going on. When he inquired what was so funny, Vi and Elaine (another long-term employee) asked him, "Who was going to fix the machines with you in a coat and tie?" Dave didn't initially realize that keeping the 80+ year old machines going was going to be a large part of his job. By the third day, his "management outfit" switched from a coat and tie to bakery whites, and it continued the entire time he held that position!

When his father passed away in 2006, Dave took over the company and runs it today. Under his guidance, the company continues to sell the Spud Bar, along with the Old Faithfull (introduced in 1925), the Cherry Cocktail Bar (introduced in 1926) and the Owyhee Butter Toffee (also introduced in 1925).

Recently, they added Huckleberry Gems to the mix, which are huckleberry-flavored marshmallow crèmes covered in milk chocolate.

The company appeals to customers seeking out the fun and excitement of candy produced in yesteryear. One of the key differences of the Idaho Candy Company, and others trying to play off of the nostalgic trend, is that their company is not imitating candy made in the past. They are making the bars they always have, in the manner they always have, via the same equipment they always have. A true bite of the past!

The company finds new accounts at the yearly Fancy Food Show in San Francisco. They exhibit and seek out new businesses looking to add an element of nostalgia to their shelves. They also use a broker network to represent their products to distributors and grocery chains in 12 states.

While steadfastly maintaining the integrity of its products, the company has continued to evolve to appeal to today's consumers and the demands of stores. They recently went through a graphic design change to their packaging and updated their cases to make them more appealing to businesses stocking them.

Their 103-year old factory recently passed an intense food safety audit necessary to go after large accounts. Many vendors demand this certification in place before they will work with companies.

The company continues to enjoy a solid base of loyal customers, a regional appreciation as well as new individuals seeking out candy from yesteryear. They occasionally benefit from free advertising on TV shows about candies of the past. The Food Network® has featured the Idaho Candy Company multiple times. Even programming outside of the food channels occasionally happens. The show *American Restoration*™ recently featured the Idaho Spud Bar on a show where Rick Dale and his team were working on an old vending machine and wanted some nostalgic candy for the restored version.

Dave Wager's plans remain pretty simple. He states, "We've been doing this for 112 years, we want to continue doing what we have done to get here."

Idaho Candy Company Photo Album

T.O. Smith (in the tie) Cooking Candy

The production line in the 1910's (T.O. is on the left)

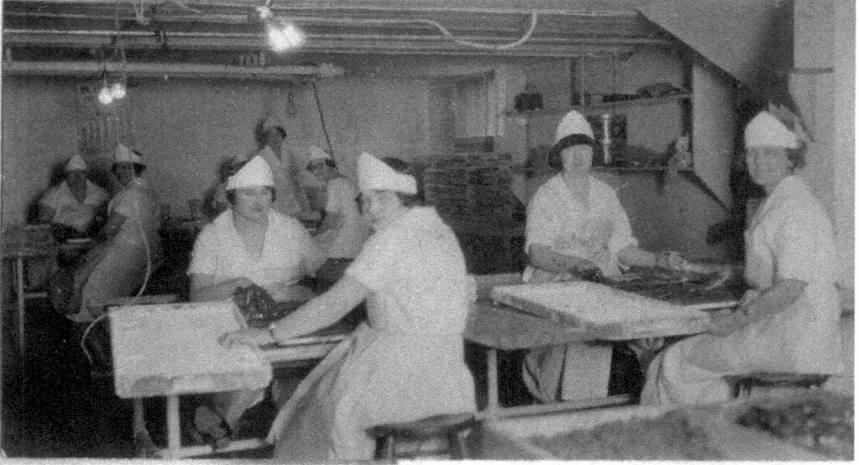

Hand-dipping in the 1920's

Making Cream Goods in the 1920's

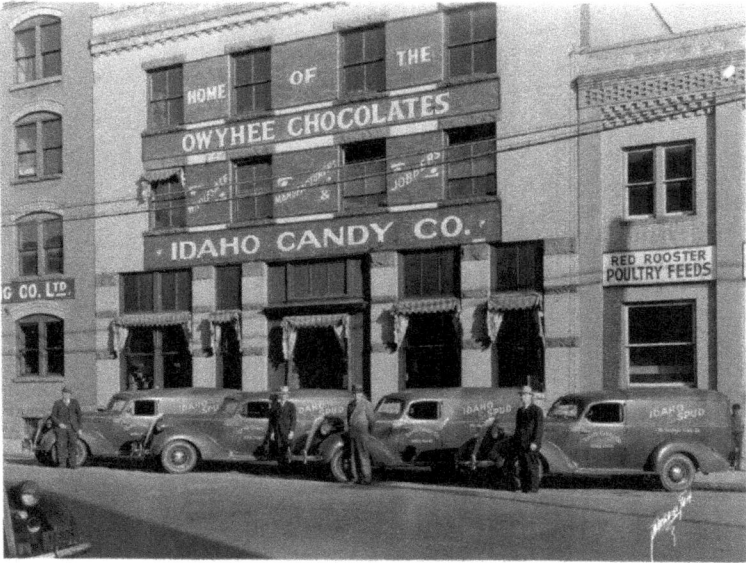

The Factory in the 1930's

Ray "the Salesman's" Car

Idaho Candy Company product lineup

Chapter 5: Coffee

Metropolis Coffee Company

1039 West Granville Avenue
Chicago, IL 60657
(773) 338-4904

metropoliscoffee.com
communications@metropoliscoffee.com

Established
2003

Leadership
Bob Quinlan, CEO

Products
Small batch artisan roasted coffee

Coffee, the bond of a family...

It's pretty safe to say that a family who owns a café and a coffee roasting/distribution company loves coffee. For Jeff and Tony Dreyfuss (father and son), the passion for coffee each started in a unique way that would ultimately bring them together.

In the late 90's, Jeff Dreyfuss was a college professor who grew to love the coffee scene of the area surrounding Seattle where he lived. He was fascinated with the care which went into roasting and making the perfect cup of coffee.

Since he would go to the same roasteria/café each day, he got to know the head roaster. Soon his new friend would allow him in the back where he got to see firsthand the preparation and process of roasting the coffee he was enjoying.

Meanwhile, halfway across the country in Wisconsin, his son Tony, graduated from the University of Wisconsin with a Philosophy degree. Unable to put his degree to work, he worked a variety of jobs in the area. Ultimately, he decided to move to the Pacific Northwest, and he landed a job at Peet's Coffee® in Portland.

Starting at an entry level position, Tony would quickly work his way up the ranks at the store. He became consumed with the industry and felt he had found his calling in life. With both Jeff and Tony actively engaged in everything coffee, it became their favorite topic of conversation when they would speak on the phone or see each other in person. In fact, they dedicated so much time to the topic of coffee, they finally decided the only way they could alleviate their obsession was to open a store together. They selected an area with a lesser coffee scene, but seemingly with more opportunities to develop: Chicago.

In 2003, Jeff and Tony opened Metropolis Coffee in the Edgewater neighborhood of Chicago. This wasn't to be just any neighborhood coffee café, though. They were not going to simply buy someone else's roasted coffee. Nor were they going to buy wholesale beans and just roast those onsite.

They were destined for much greater things than you find at your typical coffeehouse. There would be no cutting corners in search of the perfect cup of coffee. They would get their beans directly from the farmers and roast them to their own exact standards and specifications.

This was all to be done rooted in a belief that the perfect cup of coffee comes from a line of respect. That respect starts with the farmers. You must start by paying them a fair price for their harvest. You have to take great care in roasting the beans and brewing the coffee. When those standards are set, the rest seemingly would take care of itself.

Without any advertising, Metropolis Coffee quickly found a customer base. The mix was a great cross section of students from Loyola University, business people from nearby companies and locals from the area neighborhoods. Jeff and Tony made a real effort to appeal to their diversified clientele by having a variety of events in the store. They would have open mic nights, art programs featuring the works of local artists, and story time for families with children.

Not only was the experience at the café a hit, their coffee was getting rave reviews as well. The demand for product to take home to brew at customers' houses or offices was so high they decided to see if there was a market to sell Metropolis Coffee at grocery and convenience stores.

After securing a deal with Whole Foods®, Metropolis was in demand from the local grocers. Soon, Tony was focusing on getting his coffee expanded distribution to more retailers.

With Jeff gradually moving out of day-to-day operations and into the position of President guiding the company's vision and initiatives, and Tony concentrating on landing more accounts to sell their bagged coffee, they sought assistance for the business. The success Jeff and Tony had found led to a whole new set of issues they could never have even begun to imagine when they wanted to start their own roasteria and café. Now they were looking at managing a successful café and trying to take a brand national.

After completing a nationwide search for a CEO, they found the perfect candidate right in Chicago. Bob Quinlan had worked for a Metropolis competitor and had experience in growing their brand outside of the Chicago area.

Hiring Bob has allowed Tony to focus solely on selling. He is actively growing the business, and it is beginning to fan out from its Midwestern roots. Metropolis can be found in small stores, big chains and even as the house coffee for other cafés which do not do their own roasting.

 Jeff is still a constant sight for the locals used to seeing him working the counter, enjoying some small talk or simply sipping a great cup of coffee.

Despite the success, they remain the same coffeehouse they were when they opened. They still don't advertise, but they are very active in social media. A conversation started at the café very well might be continued on Facebook® or Twitter® with a Metropolis team member joining in the conversation as well. They also use social media to extend invitations to the various events they have going on at the café.

In the end, the means to their success has been exactly what Jeff and Tony used to talk about on the phone long before they opened their own business and moved to Chicago. They believed that a successful coffee business starts with a great cup. They have managed to do this by getting involved in every facet of the cup, long before it's in their store.

With their approach, it won't be long before any serious coffee drinker starts to know the name Metropolis is associated with the ultimate coffee experience. This will always be the case because Jeff and Tony stand behind every cup!

Metropolis Coffee Company Photo Album

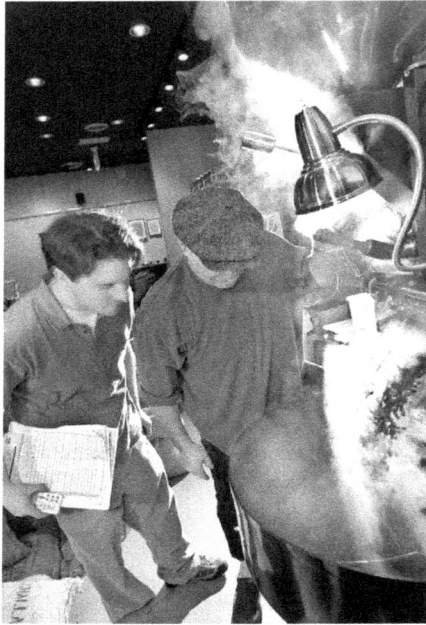

Tony and Jeff roasting a batch

Baristas hard at work at the café

Coffee beans waiting to get roasted

Working the roaster

Tony pouring a cupping

A cup of Metropolis Coffee on a train engine

Pouring a shot of espresso

Packaging bags of coffee on the line

A pour over in action

Sample of Metropolis' packaging

Chapter 6: Distilled Spirits

Great Lakes Distillery

616 W. Virginia Street
Milwaukee, WI 53204
(414) 431-8683

greatlakesdistillery.com
vodkaguy@greatlakesdistillery.com

Established
2004

Leadership
Guy Rehorst, Owner

Products
Distilled spirits

Small batch products made with old world methods...

After going through the process of turning a start-up company into a profitable business, Guy Rehorst was a little burnt out. His company, a high tech manufacturer of CDs and DVDs, had been a great experience. Starting from concept, he and his business partner had built the organization up to the point where it had become very successful. They had gone from a two-person team to a company employing 60 individuals.

With each job needing to be customized and the rigors of running the day-to-day operations of a stressful company wearing on him, Guy elected to let his partner buy him out when he expressed an interest in doing so. The cash infusion of selling the company meant Guy was afforded the luxury of being able to do exactly what he wanted to do for awhile. What he wanted to do was "nothing."

That's an overstatement, of course. He was burned out on business and relished the opportunity to spend some time with his kids. With a goal to stay out of the work force for at least a year, he began his at-home sabbatical.

During this time away from working, he was also able to pick up a hobby he hadn't had the time for in quite awhile: home brewing and wine making. As he started once again making his own wine and beer, he quickly remembered why he had liked doing so in the past. He loved the idea of working with ingredients, refining recipes and the end result of a product you could enjoy and share with friends.

When he began thinking about getting back into the working world again, he decided to take a look at his hobby. After all, doesn't everyone want to do something which they really enjoy for a living?

Beer and wine had so many competitors, he decided to explore the concept of entering the world of distilled spirits. As he started to research the idea, he was quickly concerned. Despite the fact craft distilling was just starting to take off in the U.S., there were no distillers in Wisconsin. Initially, he thought there may be laws against distilling, or at a minimum, repressive laws which made it very difficult to even try.

After checking around, he was pleasantly surprised to find out there wasn't anything legally stopping him. His concerns weren't totally alleviated, though. He still worried perhaps there were issues which he wasn't yet understanding since no one else had opened a distillery in his home state.

Was it too time-consuming?

Were the start-up costs too high?

Was dealing with federal, state and local regulations too difficult?

Jim began to visit other distillers and taking whatever classes he could on making spirits. He wanted to learn as much as he could about the industry before he jumped in. After a thorough assessment, Jim came to the realization that while there certainly would be a lot of hard work, and there are plenty of legal hurdles surrounding any sector with alcohol, creating a distillery was a viable option.

He started working on what would become Great Lakes Distillery. His initial facility was just 3,000 square feet but it represented a dream come true as he was in the craft distilling business.

Knowing vodka is the number one distilled spirit consumed in the U.S., and it has one of the shortest production times, Jim began producing it as his first product. A signature of Great Lakes Distillery today, giving their products a tie-in to its home state of Wisconsin, was present in this first product. Great Lake's vodka utilizes Wisconsin red wheat which gave their product a natural sweetness.

While he had found a landscape open to him starting a distillery, Jim did find some of the local laws challenging in terms of allowing him to truly connect with consumers. Unlike the large nationally known brands with big advertising budgets, Jim found the way to connect with his customers was via direct interaction.

By law, though, he was not allowed to sample his product, sell it onsite or mix cocktails. He began to work on state legislators to get the changes which would translate into a better consumer experience. After much hard work and a lot of time, he was able to get legislature passed which allowed on-premise sampling and sale of his product as well as the ability to mix cocktails.

Jim orchestrated the next step for Great Lakes when he moved to a modern 14,000 square foot facility, complete with a 3,500 square foot tasting room. This new home for the company allowed them to truly connect with consumers by conducting distillery tours and samplings onsite. Customers could also have a cocktail mixed for them, and if they liked the product, they could buy it right there.

Today, Great Lakes Distillery offers eight different products:

Absinthe – They offer two varieties: a traditional green, based on a classic recipe from an 1850's French distillery and a rouge based upon a Spanish recipe.

Artisan Series Brandy – The company makes a variety of fruit brandies with bold flavors. Production is based on what fresh produce is available to them at the time.

Kinnickinnic Whiskey – Great Lakes makes a blend utilizing bourbon, malt and rye whiskies. Categorized as a "young whiskey," their whiskey has received multiple awards in the blended category including the prestigious **London World Whiskey Awards**™.

Pumpkin Seasonal Spirit – Great Lakes' Pumpkin Seasonal Spirit is a pumpkin spice whiskey. It is flavored with local pumpkins and aged in oak. It is sold just in the fall and sells out very quickly.

Rehorst Citrus and Honey Vodka – Great Lakes' Citrus and Honey Vodka offering is very different than other flavored products found on retail shelves. They do not add flavorings to their final product which can either be overwhelming or change the consistency of the product (think along the lines of the syrupy offerings you find out there). Instead, they add real lemon zest and central Wisconsin honey (one of the purest in the world) during the distillation process. This adds undertones of the flavors to the final product but does not overwhelm, nor does it change the consistency of the offering. Great Lakes offers true citrus and honey vodka, not a product *flavored* to *taste* like it.

Rehorst Gin – Great Lakes' gin is a standout from its competitors based upon the 9 botanicals used to create it. Wisconsin ginseng, the highest quality ginseng in the world, and sweet basil are just a couple of the botanicals utilized to give Rehorst Gin its complex and unique flavor. Like the honey in the vodka, their botanicals are added in the distilling process, adding subtle flavor to the final product.

Rehorst Vodka – The company continues to deliver a unique taste experience for this product utilizing their local red wheat.

Roaring Dan's Rum – Long before the "maple craze" began, Great Lakes was offering their Roaring Dan's which is a maple rum. Competitors' products tend to be thick and sticky sweet. Roaring Dan's is a dry rum, not sweet at all, but does have the taste of maple. Again, this is done during the distillation process, offering true flavor for the end product.

Currently, Great Lakes Distillery's products can be found in about half of the 50 states. Guy sees continued growth for the company moving forward. They are looking to stay true to their roots: unique product offerings which are very different than what the megabrands are selling. Plus, almost 10 years in, they also have the benefit of time working for them. They have whiskey aging at various stages which opens many possibilities.

The next step of growth will likely involve a new facility. They are just about at capacity of what they can offer out of their current home.

One source of continued frustration is the fact they are not able to sell their own product. Per federal laws, all liquor must be sold through a distributor. This means that even a wholesale customer (like a grocery store or a restaurant/bar) interested in buying their product for their establishment must be put in touch with a distributor.

As a small brand, they can be forgotten by distributors catering to much larger brands. Guy has to carefully and actively manage these relationships. Choosing the wrong distributor can mean his product never makes the shelves. Even the right partner needs continuous training and information about their product so it stays at the forefront of the minds of their store reps.

Under the guidance of Guy Rehorst, the future of Great Lakes Distillery looks very bright. It will take a lot of hard work and persistence to continue the upward growth trends they have already experienced. It's easy to imagine Guy steering them in that direction, though.

After all, it's tough to get burned out when you are doing something you love!

Great Lakes Distillery Photo Album

Guy Rehorst

The tasting room at Great Lakes Distillery

GREAT
LAKES
DISTILLERY

One of Great Lakes' core values is a commitment
to green initiatives and the environment

Vodka was the company's initial product offering

Samples of ingredients from the distillery tour

Product lineup

Chapter 7: Frozen Pizza

Dogtown Pizza

8014 North Broadway
St. Louis, MO 63147
(314) 802-7001

dogtownpizza.com
info@dogtownpizza.com

Established
2006

Leadership
Rick Schaper, Owner/Operator
Meredith Schaper, Owner/Operator

Products
10 varieties of frozen pizza: Cheese, Pepperoni, Bacon Bacon,
Veggie, Sausage, Sausage & Pepperoni, Deluxe, Four Meat,
Hot Wing and Tomato Basil Garlic

Get it!! Bake it!! Eat it!!…

For Rick and Meredith Schaper, owning a restaurant seemed to be their destiny. Both had literally grown up in the industry. Rick's family knew the owner of a pizzeria. As a friend of the family, he was able to start working there part-time washing dishes at the age of eleven. It would end up being a job he would work in various capacities over the next decade.

Meredith also started in the restaurant business at a young age. When she was sixteen, her father had a heart attack. While he was off from his job recovering, Meredith went to work as a waitress to help her family make ends meet, handing her salary and tips over to the family.

Rick was a floor manager at the restaurant where the couple met. Meredith was stopping by for a bite after a baseball game. The two hit it off and ended up getting married. Both continued to work in the restaurant business with Rick either a cook or manager, and Meredith waiting tables and tending bar.

Their shared dream was to open their own restaurant, and they continued to talk about it even as they started a family. They began to reassess the idea of opening a restaurant when they had children began to foresee the potential impact of missing events like ballgames and school functions as they worked long hours, weekends and holidays.

Rick even elected to leave the business to sell cars. He was fairly successful at it but found the same issues with long hours and weekend work.

Even though he was out of the industry, his passion and love for owning a restaurant never went away. He just put it on the back burner. He continued to keep the idea stoked by utilizing the skills he learned back at the pizzeria where he had worked as a kid. Any time he had friends and family over, he would make a round of his specialty pizzas.

After the events of September 11th, new car sales began to decline significantly. The work wasn't what he thought it was going to be when he started anyway, so he quit, vowing never to work for anyone else again.

His next venture was successful right out of the gate. He had always been great at home projects so he started flipping houses. He bought his first house for $15,000. He put a little elbow grease into it and sold it for $30,000. As the economy started to slow down, leading up to the housing market crash, his ability to flip houses went away as well.

Keeping to his pact to never work for anyone else, he got the idea to bring back the dream of owning a restaurant. He knew every aspect of the business. He wasn't looking forward to the long hours, weekends and holidays, but it was something he was confident he could do well.

He spoke to the bank, but he wasn't currently employed and Meredith's jobs tending bar wasn't enough to get them credit. With three growing boys in private school, they knew they weren't going to be able to swing this project on their own.

The plan they had was to gather friends and family at a big party where they would present the idea and seek investors. As they were working on the details, one of their friends suggested they scrap the idea of a restaurant. He reminded them of all of the problems they had experienced with a restaurant, and the fact they would grow exponentially if they were the owners.

Stating that Rick "already makes the best pizza anyway," why don't they go into business selling frozen pizzas? Even though it was right there in front of them, it took a neutral third party to flip the switch on the light bulb. As soon as they heard that, Rick and Meredith knew it was going to be their true opportunity.

They kept the party date they had planned to attract investors. Instead of asking for money, though, they prepared 100 frozen pizzas to sell. They got the group together, sampled pizza, and then inquired if anyone wanted to invest in a pizza, or two, or three…

While they will never know how the meeting to solicit investors would have went, the meeting to sell pizza couldn't have gone any better. They sold all 100 pizzas and had orders in hand for another forty more.

That's how their business initially got started: creating 100 pizzas at a time. They would then sell them to friends, family and even coworkers at Meredith's job. Those individuals would then tell their friends and family, and their network grew.

Eventually, they got to the point where they wanted to try to sell some pizzas through stores and not just through their word-of-mouth group. They approached Viviano's®, a small grocery store in a historic area of St. Louis known for great Italian food called, "The Hill."

Much to their surprise, the store bought their Saran Wrap®-ped pizzas with printed envelope labels. The product looked great, but the Schapers get a good laugh now as they think about how unprofessional their packaging was. The pizza sold because you could see the quality, and the fresh ingredients piled on through the clear wrap. However, the ink on the labels would end up running as the freezer door was opened and closed throughout the day. The clear packaging to see their ingredients is still a tactic they use today; they just utilize professional food grade and not home packaging.

Those labels must have been running a lot because it seemed the doors were opened constantly. Dogtown Pizza was a success. The reorders kept coming in so the Schapers started approaching other stores. The successes kept piling up. If they could get a buyer to try their pizza, they had a new customer. It was actually that simple.

When they became too big to continue to make the pizzas out of their house, they participated in a new project in the area called, the St. Louis Incubator. The Incubator is a city-sponsored shared kitchen which provides rental space in a commercial grade kitchen for home-based food businesses wanting to take the next step in their business without having to invest in facilities on their own.

It was about this time that the USDA also came calling. Any product involving meat is subject to stringent guidelines and inspections. While never intending to do anything wrong, Rick and Meredith simply did not know all of the rules.

Thus began the long process of getting the appropriate government approvals for everything from labeling, to raw product handling, to facility inspections. A tough task to be sure, but in the end, it clearly made them a better company.

Now, Dogtown Pizza is a large facility with plenty of room for growth. The USDA makes daily inspections, and Dogtown is a business they now point to in order to showcase rules for cleanliness and food preparation. One visit to their site, and you get an incredible sense of the care and commitment which goes into each pizza.

All pies are created by hand. There are no assembly lines here. Tables are manned with 20 pizzas being worked on at a time. Each pizza is created with fresh ingredients which are being prepared in conjunction with the pizza chefs who are putting them together. Nothing is frozen. Nothing is prepared in advance. Everything is done at the same time to ensure each pizza is as fresh as possible.

After a pizza is complete, it is placed in a large stand-up freezer known as a "Flash Blaster." The Blaster quickly freezes the pie, locking in those fresh ingredients and flavors.

Frozen pizzas are then run through the wrapping machine which applies a clear wrap. Rick is adamant that the consumer has to see the actual pizza they are buying, not some marketing photo, which can be misleading, as found on the national brands. Finally, a label is applied, and it is boxed up to ship.

An onion, for example, is purchased fresh by Rick from his local provider. That day, or the next at the latest, it is sliced as the chefs are preparing the Veggie Pizza. Within 20 minutes of it being cut up, it is on the pizza and frozen in the Blaster. Those pizzas will then boxed and put together on pallets for distribution and in the grocery store in two days at the most.

From onion sack to in the consumer's home in 3 days?

It would be unheard of for any national brand to even try to make a claim like that. It's just one of the many reasons Dogtown is so popular.

Today, Dogtown Pizza continues to grow. They are still expanding in the St. Louis market. Their distributor actually shares ½ of their warehouse space so they have a symbiotic relationship and commitment to the brand. As a tribute to the companies who believed in his dream from the beginning, Rick still delivers pizza directly to the seven original stores which carried his product. Business is booming with average sales exceeding 55,000 pizzas a month just in the greater St. Louis market.

Their immediate future growth will come regionally. Markets like Kansas City or Chicago are appealing. They are taking a controlled approach, though, so they don't lose focus of the quality of their product.

The best part is that Rick and Meredith have been able to do all of this on their own, building equity in their company one pizza at a time!

Dogtown Pizza Photo Album

Rick, Meredith and their boys

All Dogtown pizzas are handmade

All ingredients are piled across the entire pizza

After each pizza is made, it spends some time in the "Flash Blaster" to get them prepared for packaging

Dogtown's Chicken Wing pizza featuring
Rick's secret hot sauce blend

Dogtown's clear packaging showcases their fresh ingredients

Chapter 8: Granola
Hudson Henry Baking Company

Hudson Henry
BAKING Co.

P.O. Box 460
Palmyra, VA 22963

hudsonhenrybakingcompany.com
hope@hudsonhenrybakingcompany.com

Established
2012

Leadership
Hope Lawrence, Founder

Products
Good News Granola in three flavors: Cashew & Coconut, Maple, Pecans & Coconut and Pecans & Chocolate

Start each day with *Good News*…

Hope Lawrence was born in North Carolina but spent the bulk of her childhood (1st grade through college) living on a farm in Virginia. After college graduation, she lived in London, New York, Washington (D.C.), and even Sydney, Australia (her husband is Australian) working in corporate Finance. Even as she doing well with her career, she dreamed of one day opening a bakery.

After Hudson, her first child, was born, she elected to shed the corporate job and become a stay-at-home mom. Free of being tied to live where she worked, she and her family moved to Australia and later to Fort Worth, Texas to be near her sister.

Right away, both she and her husband knew Fort Worth wasn't going to be their final stop. Hope longed to recreate the idyllic childhood she enjoyed living in Virginia, so they began to look for a farm there.

Not long after their second son Henry was born, they found a 10-acre former bed-and-breakfast near Charlottesville, Virginia. Best of all, it featured a commercial kitchen. That meant Hope could pursue her dream of opening a bakery without leaving the boys. She would be able to work right at home.

Everything seemed to be covered:
- ✓ Located in Virginia
- ✓ Had farmland/acreage
- ✓ The property had the bed-and-breakfast which would translate into an additional revenue stream
- ✓ The commercial kitchen afforded her the luxury of a place to start her dream business right at home

Finding your dream home doesn't mean that the process to acquire it is going to be dreamy. In fact, it can be a nightmare. That certainly was the experience for Hope. The whole process of purchasing the farm ended up taking almost a year to complete.

With the home purchase ordeal behind her, Hope then began to examine starting her business. The name of her company was a no-brainer. It would be the Hudson Henry Baking Company, named after her two boys. Deciding on a product line for the upstart business was a little more complicated.

She began to read motivational and business books, taking notes. As she reviewed her collection of positive thoughts, she started to think, "This stuff is so good, somebody should put it on the back of a cereal box so you can start your day with positive thoughts."

That was it!

Granola, baked with the highest quality ingredients, in bags with positive, motivational thoughts to start your day. Good News Granola was officially born.

In June of 2012, she began finalizing her recipe, tasting it and refining it. She was also doing all of the legal paperwork and planning involved in the starting of a new business.

One of her first orders of business was to acquire a space at the Charlottesville Farmer's Market. It is a highly successful market right in downtown Charlottesville. She thought it would be a great place to begin to showcase and sell her product. There was one small issue, though; there is up to a two-year wait to get in as a vendor.

While she didn't want to wait two-years, a delay until the next season would clearly allow her to get her business in order.

With a goal of being ready to be up-and-running by the spring of 2013, she continued to work to refine her recipes, design her logo, establish packing procedures and facilitate everything which encompasses starting a new business.

In October of 2012, she got a call from the Charlottesville Farmer's Market. They had an opening. If she was ready to go, she could secure a spot at the market.

While she wasn't "ready to go," she certainly wasn't going to miss the opportunity to participate. She quickly finalized her recipe, ordered some labels and put her packaging together. Not knowing whether or not anyone would be even be interested in her product, she took 30 bags to her first day at the market. The first person who came by sampled the product and loved it. She bought a bag. It turned out she owned a local store. She immediately inquired about carrying Hope's granola at her store. (A relationship that continues to this day... not a bad first sale!)

Hope ended up selling out that day, and, with the exception of one week, every week thereafter for the rest of the season. Since she was having so much success at the farmer's market, friends and family told her she needed to pursue more stores.

With these suggestions to expand distribution, one name in particular kept coming up. It was a gourmet food store in Charlottesville which had a large local following and a lot of tourist traffic. Being a wife, mother, starting up her business, working the farmer's market, maintaining the farm and fulfilling orders for her existing customers didn't afford Hope the luxury of the time she would need to pursue additional opportunities, so her plan for more outlets was on hold.

When she was finally to a point where she felt she was caught up enough to pursue new business, the first store she decided to contact was the gourmet food store in Charlottesville. She was surprised to find out the owner had the same name as her best friend in grade school, a girl who had moved away and lost touch. While the name wasn't common, she assumed it was simply a coincidence and never thought it could possibly be the same person.

When she placed her first call to the store owner, she was amazed to find it was in fact her old friend! The relationship was immediately rekindled, and they began working together. The store has become the most successful retailer for Good News Granola, which translates into many direct customers for Hope since so many individuals pick it up on vacation, but turn to her directly when they get back home and want more.

About the same time she was getting her products into the gourmet store, Hope was about to get some more good news. An advocate within Whole Foods® helped walk her through the paperwork to sell it at their stores. She has also helped introduce Hope to the right people within the organization to keep their relationship moving forward.

A typical day for Hope involves getting up early and baking in the morning. By lunch she is done and she spends the afternoon with her children. After dinner and time with the family, she goes back to work in the evenings from about 9:00 p.m. – 11:00 p.m. During that time, she is invoicing, preparing retail and internet orders for shipment, researching new stores to pitch and making initial contacts via email.

Email introductions, followed up with samples of her product, have proven to be a successful means for Hope to get introduced to new accounts.

While launching her granola line, she and her husband have been able to successfully renovate two of the cottages on her property. With a nearby military academy, a university with parents dropping off their children and the tourism of Charlottesville, the Lawrence's Welsummer Farm (*welsummerfarm.com*) bed-and-breakfast could turn out to be a nice form of supplemental income.

Plus, having a granola company seems to be a good fit for a bed-and-breakfast. Each customer of Welsummer has the high potential of also becoming a Hudson Henry Baking Company customer as well.

After a lot of hard work, it now appears that everything is falling in place for the Lawrence family, which is in line with the positive thinking Hope always strives for. She lives by the creed that if you think positive, and do positive things, the good karma comes back to you.

Besides the business, life itself is pretty good for Hope and family. While they do not live on a working farm, they do have some chickens, and they have the perfect setting Hope had dreamed of for raising a family.

She is flush with ideas on how to grow the business. It is so clear to her on how to make it a success it appears to be not a question of how it will happen, but when.

With a great family, a dream home on the farm and a business that is quickly building a head of steam, she speaks of one more dream: the chance to get on the *Today*™ show to talk about her granola with Kathie Lee and Hoda.

Knowing that there are tens, if not hundreds of thousands of individuals who want the same opportunity, it may seem farfetched. Then again, Hope always seems to find a way to make things happen so you never know.

Hudson Henry Baking Company Photo Album

Hope Lawrence with her sons Hudson (left) and Henry (right)

Henry and Hudson playing on the farm

My vision is to build a family business that helps others be their best. With that, I'd like to pass on these thoughts and ideas. I hope that these words improve your day (and that you truly enjoy our granola)!

HELP SOMEONE TODAY. HAVE THE BEST DAY EVER... STARTING...NOW!

Have a vision, write it down and make it happen.

Do something today to start that business/project that you have been thinking about for far too long. **PAY A COMPLIMENT.**

ASK FOR WHAT YOU WANT.

BE GRATEFUL. *Know, in your heart of hearts, that everything is possible.*

Hope Lawrence
Founder, Hudson Henry Baking Co.

NUTRITION FACTS: Serv. Size: 1/4 cup (30g) Servings Per Container: about 11, Amount Per Serving: Calories 150, Calories from Fat 80, Total Fat 9g (14% DV), Saturated Fat 4.5g (24% DV), Trans Fat 0g, Cholesterol 0mg (0% DV), Sodium 55mg (2% DV), Total Carbohydrate 14g (5% DV), Dietary Fiber 2g (6% DV), Sugars 5g, Protein 4g, Vitamin A (0%), Calcium (2%), Vitamin C (0%), Iron (8% DV). Percent Daily Values (DV) are based on 2,000 calorie diet. Your daily values may be higher or lower depending on your calorie needs.

Ingredients: Rolled oats, pumpkin seeds, cashews, coconut oil, maple syrup, coconut, brown sugar, sliced almonds, sea salt, vanilla extract, cinnamon. **This Product Contains Almonds, Cashews, Coconut.** Enjoy By:

Hudson Henry Baking Co. • 221 Palmer Country Ln.
Palmyra, VA 22963 • www.hudsonhenrybakingco.com

"Good News" from the back of the Cashew and Coconut bag

The inside of a Welsummer Farm cabin

Close-up of Good News Granola

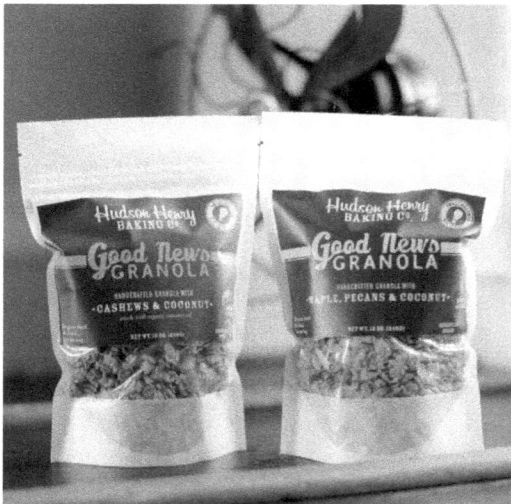

Hudson Henry product line-up

Chapter 9: Gum

Verve, Inc.

305 Dudley Street
Providence, RI 02907
(401) 351-6415

gleegum.com
info@gleegum.com

Established
1995

Leadership
Deborah Schimberg, Founder & CEO

Products
Eight flavors of all-natural gum (Triple Berry, Bugglegum, Tangerine, Peppermint, Spearmint, Cinnamon, Sugar-Free Lemon Lime and Sugar-Free Refresh-Mint) and three candy making kits (Gum, Chocolate and Gummies)

From tree to Glee…

In the scheme of things, gum has a pretty short history. In the 1880's – 1890's companies began to produce gum utilizing chicle, the sap from certain trees found in areas that would typically be defined as rainforest. At the time, all companies used chicle to produce gum, and there weren't any megabrands, only small regional players serving customers in their immediate area.

It really came into popular culture in World War II when it was included in the G.I.'s rations. Phrases like "Got some gum, chum" were used in cartoons to demonstrate the popularity of gum with soldiers. When they began to seek out chewing gum after returning home, an industry was created and megabrands began to form to meet their demand.

A constant with gum is that it is fun. It's simply a product which appears to break all boundaries of social and economic status. Adults, kids, rich and poor, everyone seems to love the experience of chewing a piece of gum.

The thought of being fun resonates through everything Glee Gum does. Whether you are looking at their packaging (they have a fun, yet cool, package and logo), corresponding with the company (customer responses are signed off, "Yours in Glee") or speaking to Founder and CEO Deborah Schimberg, everyone seems equally enthusiastic and excited to be a part of the Glee team. Not the faux enthusiasm you might find in the stiff confines of the corporate world either. We are talking 100% genuine participation into what Glee Gum is doing.

They are doing a lot, by the way. Deborah Schimberg, a Brown University graduate, started a non-profit community and urban environmental garden and educational program when she graduated from college. Her belief that business can be a solid contributor to society could already be witnessed when the group she started began an organic salad greens company under her leadership. That successful business, in-turn, helped continue to sustain the work she was doing in the community to assist in growing gardens in urban areas and communities.

She then began the second act of her career which would also play a large role into what she would eventually be doing with Glee Gum. She got into the education field. First, as a principal of a school in Costa Rica, and then later, opening a dual-language charter school.

Even though she had a passion for and immensely enjoyed the education field, she continued to have a great interest in socially responsible business. One product which particularly interested her: Ben & Jerry's® Brazilian Rainforest Crunch™. It utilized Brazil nuts from the rainforest. These were harvested by the local people of the area.

As she composed the list of everything she loved about the concept, she came up with the following:

- The nuts were obtained without damaging the rainforest
- The locals were paid a fair wage for their work in collecting the nuts
- An incentive was created not to destroy the rainforest since they were making a living off of the sustainable product
- The ice cream tasted great

It seemed to be a win anyway you looked at it!

On a trip to the rainforest of Guatemala, she accidentally discovered a way to replicate the business approach of the Rainforest Crunch™ ice cream in a totally separate type of business.

When she saw a demonstration of how the chicle from some of the indigenous trees of the area was harvested to make chewing gum, she was intrigued. Before synthetic bases were utilized, chicle was the way all gums were created. Criss-cross patterns are scored into the trunk of the trees, the sap drips out and is collected. The tree then heals with no lasting effects. They then can be harvested for chicle every 5 – 6 years.

After studying the feasibility of utilizing chicle and some work with the locals in Guatemala, she proceeded to introduce chicle back to the United States. Her first product wasn't Glee Gum, though. It was a kit to make gum. The kit was designed for kids to utilize the chicle to learn about the history of gum and to make a delicious and fun treat.

In 1995, when she introduced the gum kit, Deborah really hadn't intended to introduce a chicle-based gum on the market. She received so much interest and glowing correspondence about how tasty the gum was, in 1998 she launched Glee Gum.

Utilizing chicle wasn't the only difference in Glee versus its competitors. The list of reasons why you would want to chew Glee instead of one of the megabrands is almost overwhelming.

Some of these differences include:

- There are no genetically modified organisms (GMOs) in the product
- Glee uses no artificial colors or flavors
- It contains no artificial sweeteners like aspartame
- Classic Glee is sweetened with Fair Trade Certified cane sugar and rice syrup (not high-fructose corn syrup)
- Sugar-free flavors are sweetened with xylitol, a naturally occurring sap from birch and beech trees
- It is packaged in 100% recyclable cardboard packaging and not blister packs which end up in landfills

The best part is the gum is not only delicious; it is priced on-par with the national brands.

You would think a product with so much going for it in terms of social responsibility would scream "green," or laud the merits of its "sustainability" and positive impact on the local population in Guatemala, but it doesn't. Even though these are core values of the company, and perhaps the most important driving force behind the creation of Glee, Deborah goes back to keeping it fun.

Gum is fun. Kids love fun. The way to generate their interest in the important messaging is not to overly sell environmentalism and social consciousness; it is to first get the kids interested in a product they will love. Hence, the cool packaging Glee has put together.

Deborah's commitment to education continues with her company today as well. She currently has three candy making kits. These boxed kits are designed to be a hands-on learning experience to make delicious treats. She has the chewing gum kit, as well as chocolate and gummies kits.

She has been actively involved in making her kits not only a fun project to do at home with the family, but something which can be utilized in the classroom as well. The educational value of the kits goes far beyond learning how to make the individual candies. She has developed complete lesson plans where the kits are a fun activity and learning experience.

Imagine the fun of learning about fair trade, business, harvesting ingredients, and nutrition, all culminating with classroom time where kids get to make their own chocolate candy, gum or gummie worms? It sounds like Deborah has made learning fun as well!

Growing a brand when you can't compete in terms of advertising dollars or shelf space is challenging. Gum isn't a product consumer typically put on their grocery lists. It's a product you pick up while you are shopping at the checkout. However, those spots cost money. Glee doesn't have the funds to go after those coveted positions, nor do they have the print and TV funds the national brands do.

Instead Glee is planning to meet the demand of its niche market. There is still plenty of room to grow in the health food sector, as well as the candy aisle at the grocery store, even if they cannot get into the checkout area. As they continue to grow, the goal is to continue to make the case that they deserve to compete on an even field with the larger brands.

Under Deborah's guidance, it's hard to imagine that they won't continue to make great strides in becoming a larger presence. Not only that, they are going to have a fun time getting there!

Verve, Inc. Photo Album

Deborah Schimberg

Plant a tree.

GLEE GUM WORKS WITH TREES FOR THE FUTURE TO PLANT TREES IN CENTRAL AMERICA. IF YOU RECORD YOUR NEXT PURCHASE OF GLEE HERE, WE'LL PLANT A TREE IN YOUR NAME!

Glee Gum not only features cool retro packaging, it also touts social responsibility, like their tree planting program which helps reestablish the Rain Forest in South America

Glee Gum's website walks you through the entire gum making process (demonstrating the collecting of chicle here)

A batch of Glee Gum, ready to package

Verve's candy making kits

A look at the Chocolate Kit

Counter display

The Glee Gum lineup

Chapter 10: Honey

Atlanta Honey Company

Atlanta, GA
(404) 409-7852

atlantahoneycompany.com
info@atlantahoneycompany.com

Established
2010

Leadership
Grant Giddens, Owner

Products
Wildflower Honey, Hotlanta Honey, Sourwood Honey, Wildflower Raw Honeycomb, Honey Sticks and Honey Company Candy

Atlanta Honey Company: A small brand with over 15 million employees...

While in college at Valdosta State University, Grant Giddens began to take a serious look at starting his own business upon graduation. Not only did the economy and job outlook seem bleak, he simply didn't like the idea of working for someone else. They controlled your paycheck, and in many instances, it didn't seem like the amount of hard work you put into something necessarily paid you back at an equitable share. Plus, his father had run a successful company so an entrepreneurial spirit was likely in his blood.

At school, he studied business management and was an active participant in Students in Free Enterprise (SIFE). This extracurricular activity helps prepare students for running his or her own business by engaging local leaders to provide guidance for being socially responsible business owners.

As graduation neared, he began to explore ideas for his post-graduation business. The answer to his quest actually came pretty quickly. He had a family friend who knew a lot about commercial beekeeping, and Grant had been a hobbyist himself, keeping a few hives to produce honey for himself, friends and family while in school.

With some seed money from his father, Grant got together more hives, commercial grade bottles and the appropriate federal and State of Georgia approvals to start his business.

With all of this in place, he was now officially in business at the Atlanta Bee Company. His vision was to sell a locally made product which focused on delivering a quality product which retained the health benefits of honey by keeping it natural. He wasn't going to go through the filtration process which the national companies do as they add fillers and round out their product with high fructose corn syrup. His goal was pretty simple: he aimed to sell honey and not "honey" (which is how some of the Chinese and Brazilian products on the market should actually be labeled since they are more flavored corn syrup than honey).

Initially, he started out as a one-man operation selling his product roadside out of the back of his truck. Customer feedback was so strong, he began to feel confident enough to take the next step of getting his products in the stores alongside the nationally known brands. Grant hired a food broker to begin introducing his honey into store distribution.

It would be nice to say it was smooth sailing from this point on, but in reality it couldn't be further from the truth. Grant was about to experience some major issues which could have broken the spirit of many small business owners.

First of all, the distribution via the food broker wasn't going well. They didn't have the buy-in or vision Grant did. They were successful getting his honey on the shelves, but it was sold as a premium product. The profits were bartered out of it in exchange for getting it on the shelf. While the store and broker may have been combining for profits of $5 - $6 per bottle, Grant was making well under a dollar.

The second difficult issue which came up is he actually got sued by a competitor for the name of his company. This competitor felt the Atlanta Bee Company was too close to their own name.

Grant had a lawyer review his case. He was told that clearly he was on solid footing to take the case to court, but it was going to cost thousands of dollars. This was money he clearly didn't have since he was struggling to make ends meet with his food broker deal.

With that, Grant checked his intestinal fortitude and made a few key decisions which would thankfully begin a rapid turnaround for him. First, he changed his name to the Atlanta Honey Company. Even though he was early in his business venture, being forced to change his company name was tough, especially because he was told the lawsuit was without merit.

Reflecting on this decision later, he would reassess and actually be glad it happened. As the Atlanta Bee Company, it seemed he was constantly fielding calls from confused consumers looking to buy beekeeping equipment. The Atlanta Honey Company ended up being a much better descriptor of his company, and he was pleased he made the change.

The second key moment for his new company came when he fired his food broker and elected to assume that duty. He wasn't going to allow another company to introduce his product to distributors and stores. He was going to handle all of it himself. He was the creator of the company, and he was going to be the face of it for potential partners as well.

Coming out of his darkest moments, Grant was able to pull himself and his company back up, and it really began to take off from that point forward. He became active in local farmer's markets and fairs handing out samples. He started to meet face-to-face with some of the chains he had been in with the broker and was able to get back in based on the quality of his product, not because he was giving away all of his profits. He even started working some corporate events where some of the large companies in Atlanta would entertain clients and offer local products to them while they were in town.

It was at some of these events where he started to develop some partnerships to co-market his products with other companies. He got a local popsicle company to feature his honey in one of their popsicles. A steak house utilized his honey in some of its recipes.

The most rewarding of these partnerships to date came from an Atlanta-based ice cream company. They offered a flavor called Atlanta Honey Company Ricotta Pistachio™. His logo was co-branded right on the packaging. The ice cream company has featured it at many of their trade shows, and it has even garnered interest from such well known entities as the Food Network® and the team from Oprah Winfrey's magazine "O"™.

With about two-thirds of all food dependent on the pollination of bees, the honeybee plays a vital role in a healthy ecosystem. When asked about how he "makes" honey, Grant often laughs as he states, "The bees make the honey, I just collect it." He often accentuates the point by noting he may be the biggest employer in Atlanta with all of the bees he keeps busy!

Of course, there is more to Grant's role than simply collecting honey. In a world of climate change and pollution he has to keep his bee colonies healthy. This is done primarily by securing hives in remote locations, preferably in higher altitudes. The mountainous regions provide better conditions for the bees, and there are less humans around. Grant notes that something as simple as an open soda left on a bench can be a real problem for a beekeeper. The bees are attracted to the sugar in the soda. The can, and its contents, are loaded with impurities which would be brought back to the hive.

Grant circumvents these issues by having his hives in remote locations far from people and their soda cans! He has about 300 hives, all within a 125-mile radius of Atlanta, keeping it a local honey for the community. Doing this gives Atlanta residents the added advantage of enjoying a honey which has been shown to have health benefits for those dealing with allergies from the local flora.

Currently, the Atlanta Honey Company offers the following products:

Wildflower Honey – This is honey from bees pollinating from the 200+ wildflowers that can be found in Atlanta. This is the best product for those looking for relief from allergens. Grant also has singers swear by the fact it keeps their voices strong as they are performing.

Sourwood Honey – This is one of the rarest honeys. During the last two weeks of July and first week of August, the Sourwood Trees are in bloom. These rare trees only grow along the Appalachian Mountains. The bees who are in the hives around these trees produce a purple-tinted, dark honey which has a rich buttery taste. Due to its limited scope and short season, this is Grant's most highly sought after honey. In fact, he fielded a call from a company in Tokyo this year who offered him $100,000 to buy his entire production. He took another call from a national competitor who wanted to do the same thing. While it is very difficult to turn down a check for $100,000, Grant realized he would have lost his brand equity had he done that. He would have simply been a wholesaler to another distributor who would have put their name on his unique product. He politely refused their offers and sold his Sourwood Honey to his customers.

Honey Sticks – These 6"-sticks of honey in a straw have a few uses. Some like them as a stirrer for coffee. They flavor the coffee with the honey and then mix it in with the stick. Athletes also like these because honey provides a boost of energy while they are exercising. Rather that utilizing a high-sugar energy gel, more runners are enjoying this natural approach which can provide a healthy 2-hour energy boost.

Raw Comb Honey – You may have seen the honey with the comb in it before. Did you know this is one of the greatest of the so-called "super-foods?" The comb is packed with vitamins and antioxidants which help boost the immune system. Grant notes that if you were reduced to eating only one thing in your life, Raw Comb Honey might be a great selection based on the health benefits it offers.

Hotlanta Honey – This is Grant's newest product, and it is already drawing rave reviews and winning awards. Hotlanta Honey pairs the great taste of honey with the kick of chili peppers. Chefs are raving about using the hot and sweet married together in their cooking. Grant even recently won the *Best of Georgia 2013*™ award for this product which means it is the best honey/barbecue sauce/hot sauce in the state of Georgia!

Grant's five-year plan is to have his product available around the nation. He notes that most of the work ahead for him is simply education. He knows his product is better than that of his competitors. He needs to simply create an awareness that honey doesn't come out with a perfect orange/yellow hue in a cute bear-shaped bottle. The honey might be a darker color, or it may have specs of pollen in the bottle.

No, the real value of honey is the taste and health benefits. That is something that Grant Giddens and his Atlanta Honey Company have managed to deliver on perfectly!

Atlanta Honey Company Photo Album

Grant Giddens

The Atlanta Honey Company team

Working some of the hives

Grant (center), winning a **Flavor of Georgia** award (Georgia Governor Nathan Deal is on the left) for his Hotlanta Honey

The Flavor of Georgia 2013 Award and Hotlanta brand logo

Atlanta Honey Company's product lineup

Chapter 11: Hot Sauce
Brother Bru-Bru's

P.O. Box 2964
Venice, CA 90294
(310) 396-9033

brobrubru.com
info@brobrubru.com

Established
1992

Leadership
Bruce Langhorne, Founder
Cynthia Riddle, Owner

Products
Brother Bru-Bru's Original African Hot Pepper Sauce, Brother Bru-Bru's Organic Chipotle Pepper Sauce and Brother Bru-Bru's Organic Chili Pepper Sauce

The perfect "Bru"…

A popular ad campaign for a beer company features a character known simply as "the most interesting man alive." Rather than creating a character, casting the part and writing a fictitious biography, they should have simply contacted Bruce Langhorne.

You can clearly make a strong case that Bruce is, in fact, the most interesting man alive. Take a look at these compelling facts:

- He played at the Lincoln Memorial leading up to Dr. Martin Luther King's "I Have a Dream" speech.

- Bruce was one of the most important session recording folk rock artists of the 1960's. The musicians he recorded with include Bob Dylan, Richie Havens, Joan Baez, Peter, Paul and Mary, Gordon Lightfoot and many more.

- The song *Mr. Tambourine Man* is a tribute by Bob Dylan to Bruce who used to play a Turkish drum outfitted with bells which provided a tambourine sound.

- He composed a number of movie soundtracks, including *Hired Hand* and *Swing Shift*.

- He, and his wife Janet, owned a macadamia nut farm in Hawaii.

- Bruce formed the Venice Beach Marching Society after Hurricane Katrina to be in solidarity with the people of Louisiana. He wore an elaborate headdress and joined with a group of his musician friends who played and marched up-and-down on Venice Beach.

That's just the opening arguments for his case of being "the most interesting man alive."

Another story adding to Bruce's legend is Brother Bru-Bru, the hot sauce company he formed in 1992. Bruce's rock-n-roll lifestyle caught up with him in his 50's when he was diagnosed with high blood pressure. Part of the new healthy lifestyle he had to commit to was to cut out salt.

Removing sodium from your diet is challenging for anyone, but Bruce had a particular fondness for spicy foods and hot sauce. As he began to pay more attention to labeling, he quickly realized hot sauces are loaded with sodium. There wasn't a product he could find which would meet his new commitment to health.

Since he couldn't find anything on the market, Bruce, an avid cook, decided to develop something himself. He enlisted Cynthia Riddle, an old friend from a meditation class, who had experience with formulations in the natural products business, to help him out.

Cynthia and Bruce worked to utilize all natural ingredients, without adding salt or sugar to flavor. Eventually, they got the correct mixture of peppers and African spices. It was the perfect "Bruce's Brew," so it became Brother Bru-Bru.

Bruce began to distribute his product to health food stores and specialty stores. Eventually, they were picked up by food distributors. The company actually received nationwide distribution via this method. Working through health and specialty distributors makes it difficult to know all of their customers since they are in more than 1,000 stores nationwide and the distributors have the interface with the stores. As such, the company is often surprised via customer feedback to find out where Brother Bru-Bru's is being sold.

The letters and later emails Brother Bru-Bru's receives are always encouraging. So many people, like Bruce, suffer from high blood pressure. It is an incredible moment for them when they find a hot sauce without sodium. Individuals often mention the loss of flavor on a sodium free diet and the fact that Brother Bru-Bru's allows them to add tastes they enjoy back into their food.

Bruce continued to be the face of Brother Bru-Bru's, if not the whole company, all the way until the mid-2000's. A stroke in 2006, left him unable to run the company he had started. Without Bruce, it looked like the business would either be sold (losing the commitment to healthy, natural ingredients with Bruce's name/face on the bottle was a concern) or be forced to close its doors.

Bruce's old friend Cynthia Riddle from his meditation class came to the rescue. She purchased the company with a vow to expand distribution. Bruce was retained in a chairman-emeritus type of role where he maintains a presence as the face of the brand.

In order to expand, they decided to add a few more flavors. Since Brother Bru-Bru's Original African Sauce was a natural, healthy sauce, she wanted to take the next step by making the new items organic.

The new products developed were Chipotle, the popular smoked pepper, and Warm Chili Pepper, which retained the beloved flavor profile of the Original Brother Bru-Bru's but reduced the heat. Both of these products were organic and maintained the company's commitment to healthy alternatives in the sector.

Entering the hot sauce business has proved challenging for Cynthia. There are over 1,000 competitors in this category. Simple ingredients and production translate to it being relatively easy for individuals to enter the market.

Even with such a competitive landscape, Cynthia knew her products have tremendous advantages over her competition. The combination of the health benefits, commitment to natural ingredients, no sodium, no sugar, on top of Bruce's unique personal story, means that she has a winner on her hands.

Cynthia began to draw upon her success in the natural products segment to expand the reach of Brother Bru-Bru's. She personally called on health food stores to expand shelf space.

She also looked to other areas outside of the normal channels to gain distribution for Brother Bru-Bru's. She began to market to restaurants and country clubs with her rationale being it is not only good business to sell to these entities, but also they are an introduction to potential customers for personal purchase. If someone is at their favorite restaurant and they are enjoying a meal flavored with her hot sauce, they are much more likely to seek out that brand in the store since they have already tried it.

Another creative idea Cynthia has been focusing on recently is shared sampling stations at stores. Grocery stores typically charge a company $75 - $100 to demo a product in-store. Cynthia knows that having someone try her product is a key to getting them to buy it.

The cost of $75 - $100 translates to the need for a lot of hot sauce being sold in the razor-thin margins of the grocery industry. Plus, those $100 bills start adding up very quickly as you try to make any type of significant impact by doing multiple stores or a chain.

Cynthia's idea was to have several companies split the cost of the demo personnel since there isn't an additional charge to have multiple vendors; the stores simply charge on a "per sample station" basis.

Successfully pulling the plan together simply involved legwork. Cynthia needed to call other companies she thought might be a good fit. In her mind, a shared sampling might contain Brother

Bru-Bru's with an organic chip company to serve it on and a cold beverage.

As she made her calls, she was pleasantly surprised at how many companies were willing to work with her. Best of all, not only did this reduce her cost, in most cases it was eliminated. She was able to find some larger brands who liked the idea of her coordinating the sampling, and they had budgets in place to cover the cost.

Cynthia's proudest accomplishment isn't even one which translates into product being sold (well, at least not very much), but runs along the lines of personal satisfaction. She long had a dream of getting her product into the White House since Michelle Obama is very committed to healthy eating.

Plus, she figured, Mrs. Obama is friends with Oprah, who's friends with Doctor Oz... Who knows where an introduction to Michelle Obama might lead? Of course, getting a sample of a food product to President or Mrs. Obama, for obvious reason, is not allowed by Secret Service.

Then a year ago, she was doing a small food show at the naval base in San Diego…

Along with many other vendors, she was sampling her hot sauce, hoping to drum up some interest in Brother Bru-Bru's. Late in the day, most of the vendors had either left or were packing up. She had made the two-hour trip from Venice so she had decided she was going to stay until the last person left.

With few vendors still in place, a gentleman approached the booth. He started asking questions about her product. She told him about the healthy alternative they offer at Brother Bru-Bru's. He then sampled it and complimented her on a great-tasting sauce.

It was then she noticed his badge said, "Presidential Food Detail." When she inquired as to exactly what that meant, he informed her that he was responsible for stocking the White House kitchen!

As anyone would be, she was thrilled about the prospect of having her product at the White House. The gentleman informed her that even if it were to happen, all product labels would be removed. This is done so as to not show favoritism or a means of advertising for the companies. Foods like hot sauce would have no label, but instead a generic label added that simply stated, "hot sauce."

While it was a little disheartening to know she would lose her branding, it was still flattering to know Brother Bru-Bru's would be in the White House if selected.

A few weeks later she checked back in with her contact from the Presidential Food Detail. He confirmed that Brother Bru-Bru's is now offered at the White House.

Looks like the most interesting man in the world's story just got yet even more interesting!

Brother Bru-Bru's Photo Album

Bruce and his famous tambourine which now
resides at the Seattle Music Experience®

Cynthia and Bruce working the Expo West Food Show in 1993

Bruce in his Venice Beach Marching Society headdress

Bruce Langhorne, Carolyn Hester, Bob Dylan and Bill Lee

Bruce and Cynthia today

Brother Bru-Bru's product lineup

Chapter 12: Ice Cream

Mercer's Dairy

13584 NYS Route 12
Boonville, NY 13309
(315) 942-2611
(866) Mercers (637-2377)/Toll Free

mercersdairy.com
mercersdairy@gmail.com

Established
2001

Leadership
Dalton W. Givens, Chief Operating Officer

Products
Thirty-six flavors of premium ice cream including a line of six different wine ice creams: Riesling, Red Raspberry Chardonnay, Peach White Zinfandel, Port, Chocolate Cabernet and Cherry Merlot

How about a *"glass"* of ice cream…

Mercer's Dairy was founded in 1945 by the Mercer family as a working dairy farm providing milk to the area surrounding Boonville, New York. The small Adirondacks' town is nicknamed "The Snow Capital of the East." Its hearty (read snowy) winters result in the cows producing milk with a higher butterfat content than you might find in milder climates. The average content for cows in the area is approximately 3.85% butterfat. For comparison, whole milk is 3% butterfat.

Not wanting to waste a valuable commodity, by the 1950's, the Mercers had started producing ice cream. As word of their superior ice cream started to spread, the company began to expand its reach through local grocery stores, mom and pop operations and "dip stores" where individuals would purchase ice cream cones or sundaes.

With ice cream sales expanding to a 100-mile radius around Boonville, and with the emergence of larger local dairies, the Mercers quit selling milk and focused solely on selling ice cream by the mid-1960's.

When the Mercer family decided to retire all together in 2001, nine local farm families went in as a group to purchase the business. That team, collectively known as Quality Dairy Farms, kept the Mercer name for consumer recognition with a "doing business as" Mercer's Dairy designation.

Roxaina Hurlburt was a life-long farmer and one of the individuals in the Quality Dairy Farms group which owned Mercer's Dairy. While other members of the group continued to be more focused on the day-to-day tasks of running their individuals farms, Roxaina poured her passion into focusing on the Mercer's Dairy business. She often represented the company at community events and organized affairs.

She was very active with was a group called, "Pride of New York." This group focuses on and promotes products made in

New York. Participation often means you are sampling your product to create awareness about your brands.

She began seeing some of the same people at these events and soon had many friends within the organization. Some of these friends included individuals from some of the many wineries domiciled in New York.

Out of curiosity initially, they began to pour wine over her scoops of vanilla ice cream. They were amazed at how well the flavors paired. Roxaina thought they might be onto something, and she was able to validate her findings by having many of the attendees try the pairings as well. The feedback was always overwhelming positive.

After consulting with the Wine and Grape Foundation (local wine producers) for ideas about appropriate pairings, she began to experiment with recipes. After numerous batches and tweaking of ingredients, she had a product she thought was ready for consumers.

During the holidays, she was visiting family in the Southern Tier of New York State, where she pulled out her Peach White Zinfandel ice cream. Roxaina's niece was so impressed with the flavor and uniqueness of the offering, she immediately wanted to join Roxaina in getting this product on the market. Roxaina's niece also brought in her partner, Dalton Givens, who had an extensive investment background after a thirty-year career in the financial services industry.

The timing simply could have not been better. One of the nine families was actually looking to leave the group so there was the potential for a new investor to join. Additionally, Roxaina had been struggling with partners who were a little removed from the business. She clearly needed the support and a partner who had her vision. Her niece and Dalton could provide much needed teamwork, as well as a different set of business skills to help her to bring this new line to the market.

It is possible to find wine-flavored ice cream. Nobody had a product like Roxaina had developed, though. Her Wine Ice Cream has 5% alcohol by volume, so it retains the full flavor of the wine (not flavorings designed to *taste like* wine). While this was the key to establishing a super-premium product with the true flavor of wine, it also put them in the precarious position of having to define exactly what their product was: was this an alcoholic beverage or was it a food item?

Being categorized as an alcoholic beverage would mean a whole different level of restrictions, rules and taxes. Clearly establishing wine ice cream as a food meant working with regulators to ensure it was recognized as such.

Roxaina credits persistence, and a great lawyer, in getting this accomplished. This was no small feat, mind you. It involved working with lawmakers who ultimately garnered the involvement of New York Senator Hillary Rodham Clinton to assist in developing what became known as "Mercer's Law," which firmly categorized Mercer's Wine Ice Cream as a food and not an alcoholic beverage. Now, the door opened for Mercer's Dairy to begin selling their product in stores directly to consumers.

Their biggest break, in terms of sales to-date, came in 2008 at the Fancy Food Show in New York. Their booth prominently featured their wine ice creams which always generated a lot of interest. One of the individuals who stopped by had a sample. Then he asked for another flavor. Then another. Before he left, he had tried all four of the wine ice creams offered at that time.

The next day he returned with a list of questions about the product. The day after that, he returned with a group of people who were his customers, and he wanted them to try Mercer's Wine Ice Cream. When his focus group rated it off the charts, he formally introduced himself as a global distributor and wanted to get a contract put together that day.

With a diverse portfolio which includes consumer items from such large brand names as Kelloggs®, Nestle® and Coca-Cola®, Mercer's is now his lead item to present to potential customers. His global reach means you can find Mercer's Wine Ice Cream in such far-reaching places as Asia, the Caribbean and Europe.

Despite the vision and business acumen of Dalton, Roxaina, and her niece, they were struggling with the remaining owners who did not want to invest the type of financial support needed to roll out this new brand. In early 2013, Roxaina and her niece bought out the other owners to bring back Mercer's to what had been so successful in the past, a single-family business. She, along with both her niece and Dalton, began the quest to get Mercer's as well known in the United States as it was quickly becoming globally thanks to the hard work of the distributor they had met at the Fancy Food Show.

In addition to selling through retail stores, Mercer's markets directly to consumers through a dairy store connected to their ice cream factory. Their store sells a complete line of dairy and locally made goods in addition to ice cream. At the store, consumers can order up any of the flavors Mercer's produces and/or buy flavors and sizes they cannot find anywhere else but there.

Finding new customer at the local level often means one-on-one connections facilitated through samples. Mercer's has a long-term relationship with a company which samples their product in-store for customers.

One of their greatest means of reaching individuals directly has been social media. Pinterest® in particular has been a tremendous means of finding new customers. One mention on the site led to five different appearances on TV as well as numerous mentions in newspapers and magazines!

It hasn't been uncommon for someone to post information about Mercer's Wine Ice Cream on Pinterest® and within a day to have 100 internet orders of 6 pints of Wine Ice Cream which is shipped out overnight on dry ice. People seem inherently curious about the pairing of wine and ice cream, and the superior product has ensured repeat business when new customers do find them.

Today, Mercer's continues to be known for their premium and super-premium ice creams. In fact, the recipes utilized for their classic flavors were developed in the 1950's by the Mercer family.

Their store provides a means to connect directly with consumers. In addition to a full line of dairy products, their own ice creams and soft serve, they offer other small local companies an opportunity to sell their products. The store is open all year, though business spikes during the traditional summer ice cream months.

Finding new distributors in the U.S. is one of their greatest challenges. They continue to expand slowly developing relationships over time with regional distributors. They have found the larger distributors to be ambivalent about trying to assist in growing a startup product. They simply want to fulfill orders from well-established brands with automatic orders from a public educated by large advertising budgets of the nationally known megabrands.

Through the distributors with whom they have developed relationships, their products are on shelves as far west as Texas. With a butterfat content of 13% for their regular flavors and 15% for the Wine Ice Cream, they fall under the super-premium category (compared to a 10% butterfat content typically found in well-known national competitors' products).

This limited distribution in the U.S. is in stark contrast to the product which can be found in Japan, China, The Netherlands, The Ukraine, Haiti, Singapore, Indonesia, Trinidad and much more through their global distributor.

Mercer's has successfully navigated the legal hurdles and can now sell their product in 45 of the 50 U.S. states. With the handful of states banning such items as liquor-filled chocolates, it is unlikely they will ever be in all 50, but it clearly is a significant accomplishment to secure the 90% they have.

It still amuses the Mercer's team to participate in trade shows and community events and introduce Wine Ice Cream to potential customers. The reaction tends to always be the same. They are extremely enthusiastic about the product and have a high desire to try it. Once they do, the Mercer's team claims their positive feedback is at 100%!

While Mercer's has long been out of the dairy cow business, upstate New York continues to be an excellent place to establish an ice cream business. There are many yogurt manufacturers in the area, and they do not utilize the butterfat in their product. Just like the Mercer family in the 1940's, today's farmers in the area have found an abundance of butterfat on their hands. The team at Mercer's is glad to have this easy access for something so important to their core business.

With new single-serving product sizing coming, ideas for other alcohol-based ice creams, the passion of Roxaina Hurlburt and her niece as well as the business savvy of Dalton Givens, the name Mercer's Dairy seems poised to soon become firmly entrenched in the minds of the ice cream buying public.

Mercer's Dairy Photo Album

The Mercer's crew working the New York Fancy Food Show

Mercer's dairy/ice cream shop

A busy summer night at Mercer's

A soft serve cone from Mercer's

The giant Adirondack chair at Mercer's Dairy

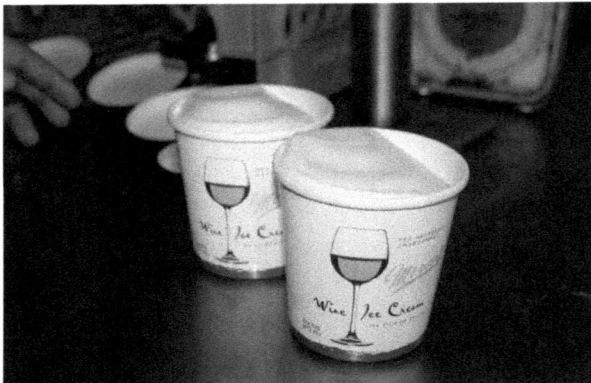

Production of Mercer's Wine Ice Cream

Chapter 13: Jams & Jellies

The Nashville Jam Company

112 McGavock Pike
Nashville, TN 37214
(615) 423-2462

thenashvillejam.com
sales@thenashvillejamsco.com

Established
2010

Leadership
Cortney Baron, Owner

Products
Jams in the following flavors: strawberry, blackberry, blueberry, raspberry, mango pineapple, cranberry marmalade, peach brandy, raspberry jalapeno, strawberry jalapeno, peach habanero, three pepper (mild heat), jalapeno (medium heat), six pepper (hot)

Nashville jams and their jam rocks…

Cortney Baron, owner of the Nashville Jam Company, may be one of the few people with anything good to say about the 2008 downturn in the U.S. economy. Yes, it initially hit home and negatively impacted her family like it did so many others, but out of the turmoil, The Nashville Jam Company was born.

The parents of two children, Cortney, who was in marketing at the time, and her husband Gary began to struggle financially when Gary's income as a manufacturer's sales rep began to drop as the economy slowed. They decided to get creative and grow their own tomatoes on a piece of property Gary's parents owned.

With no farming experience, they planted 400 tomatoes plants at the family property. When the fruit started coming in, Gary and Cortney began going to farmer's markets to sell their tomatoes.

Despite the fact business was going incredibly well, they still had more tomatoes than they could sell. They decided to get creative and utilize some of their stock as homemade salsas. They devised two recipes, a watermelon salsa, which was mild and a hot salsa called cherry bomb.

The diversification was paying off. People began to not only buy the salsa, but tomato sales went up as well. The idea of developing a product, marketing it and selling it seemed to be a feasible idea with the success they were experiencing in their first season selling at a farmer's market.

To be successful, they knew they needed to go beyond tomatoes and salsa. The Barons wanted to create something that they could sell the entire year and not just when it was in season.

Utilizing some old family recipes, and experimenting on their own, Cortney and Gary began producing homemade jams. Right away, they knew they had a winner on their hands when their first batch sold out immediately. They made some more jam and headed back to the farmer's market, and the jams sold out again.

This process happened over-and-over again with their jams selling out long before the tomatoes each time they set-up at a market. Before long, they decided to get out of the tomato and salsa business and focus solely on the jams.

Initially, the jam company was a sideline opportunity for the family. Cortney and Gary had a Domestic Kitchen Permit from the U.S. Department of Agriculture, and they processed, cooked and poured every jar of their jams at their home kitchen. Utilizing this approach, they could continue staying busy and selling at the farmer's market, but their capacity was limited.

There came a time when they simply realized they were at a crossroad with the business. Cortney still had her marketing job, and eventually Gary's sales began to pick up again in his job. They were totally maxed out with what they could produce in their home kitchen, and they still weren't meeting customer demand. For the Baron family, it was time to either jump in full bore and take a run at establishing a jam company, or they simply had to shut down production and walk away.

With all indicators pointing to The Nashville Jam Company having a bright future, the Barons decided it was too good of an opportunity to pass up. Cortney quit her job in marketing and in

2010 The Nashville Jam Company had officially transitioned from hobby to passion for the Barons.

The name obviously comes from their hometown, but the Barons were excited about the thought of Nashville's rich music history being tied to their product via the word "jam." They came up with the name and began to research it assuming it wouldn't be available. When it was, they locked-in on it as their official company name.

Entering the food business can be a daunting task for anyone. As you can imagine, there are plenty of rules and regulations, as well as plenty of forms and paperwork to fill out. Starting a business yourself, you almost have to bump your way through via trial and error. The Barons are quick to point out some of the help they got through the local office of the Department of Agriculture was invaluable in getting their business going.

One of the nice aspects to running the business has been working with the growers. With the exception of peaches which they get in Georgia, the rest of the fruit in their jams comes from their home state of Tennessee. The Barons note the growers have been great to work with, and they are very appreciative of their business.

They do have to stay on top of their inventories, though. One time Cortney notes Gary had to be sent to Florida when they ran short of strawberries. She states, "We buy all of our fruit in season locally. If you don't plan accordingly, or if we get a much bigger order than expected, you have to do things like that to fulfill our commitments."

Today, their kitchen is finally back together. They process, cook and jar their jams and jellies at a manufacturing facility. Cortney serves as president of the company, and Gary continues to work his sales job, but does help out in his spare time.

In addition to Cortney and Gary, the company has five employees, each bringing something to the table. Two are actually growers who produce some of the fruit and help out with production with Cortney during the day. Having them involved ensures that Cortney is available to make sales calls, work on account maintenance and manage the business beyond just cooking jams and jellies.

The company's other three employees allow the company to continue to focus on its roots: farmer's markets. The Nashville Jam Company's team can fan out and work the farmer's markets where product demonstrations, one-on-one discussions and taste tests are what wins customers.

Without fail, individuals who try their products always go back to a variation of one statement: "It tastes like what my mom, or my grandma used to make." Individuals tend to be amazed that a product in a jar and sold at grocery stores can bring them back to the tastes of their childhood.

One of the lucky pieces of business for the company is a focus on "grower's markets" in the greater Nashville area. At these markets you cannot just set-up and sell any products. While some farmers markets have almost become outdoor grocery stores, a grower's market limits items which can be sold to either products you produce or grow yourself. The Nashville Jam Company's products really stand out, and individuals are amazed when a company owner talks to them about a jam they produced themselves.

Their success in selling directly to consumers has also led to opportunities at some of the nation's largest chains. The Nashville Jam Company is already represented in the southeast region for one large retailer and a chance meeting with the right person at another has secured a place in a second large chain.

When a new grocery store opened not far from their home, Cortney and Gary happened to be there and started speaking to the manager. He liked the idea of their product and made a call to his district manager who covers the southeastern portion of the U.S. That call has landed them a deal to secure product placement in 19 of the company's stores with an opportunity to expand in more stores if their product sells.

When Cortney talks about the future of the company, it's a funny moment when she discusses her dreams for the future. She believes they will transition slowly from a local provider to a regional company. From there, they should steadily build to being a nationwide product. For her, the ultimate would be for her family in New York to be able to go to the store and pick up a jar of her jam (cue the awkward "record scratching sound," and shout in unison like the old Pace® salsa commercials: "New York City?").

It's true.

The driving force behind The Nashville Jam Company is actually a New York transplant. Don't give her too hard of a time, though, after all, sales are "jammin'!"

The Nashville Jam Company Photo Album

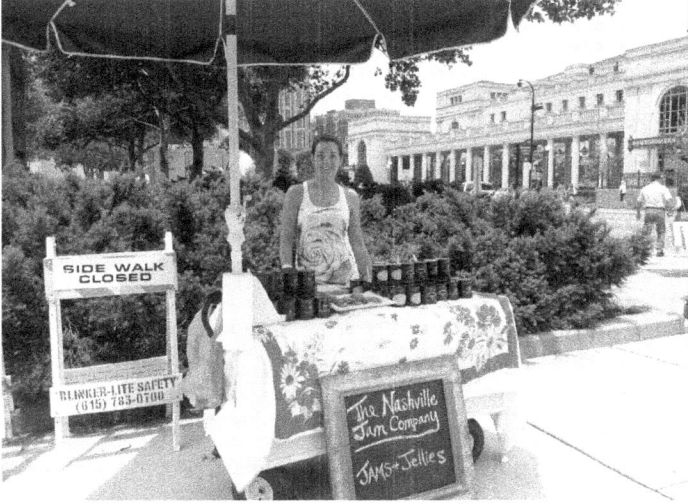

Cortney Baron sampling product at the
Country Music Awards Festival in Nashville

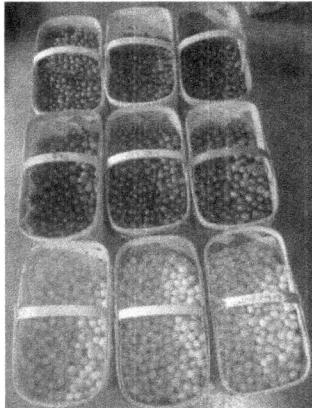

Fresh fruits ready to be made into jam

Soon-to-be-famous April McKinney makes cooking videos on YouTube® using The Nashville Jam Company's products

A look at The Nashville Jam Company's label

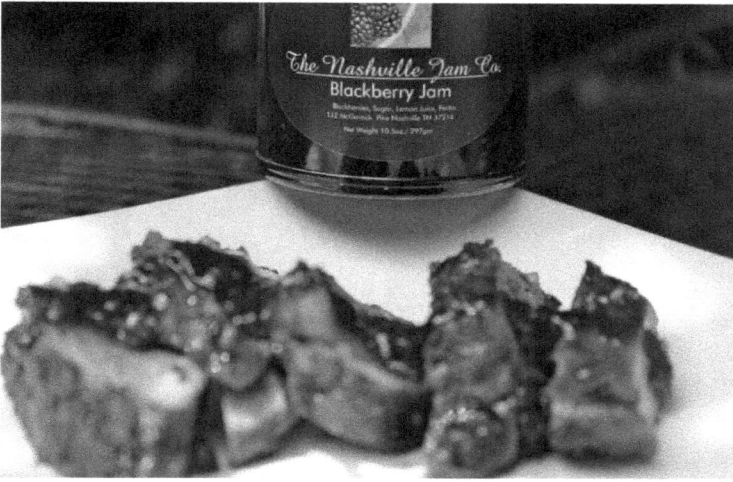

Using their Blackberry Jam to cook tenderloin

Photo shoot from their Strawberry Vinaigrette recipe

Six pepper jelly

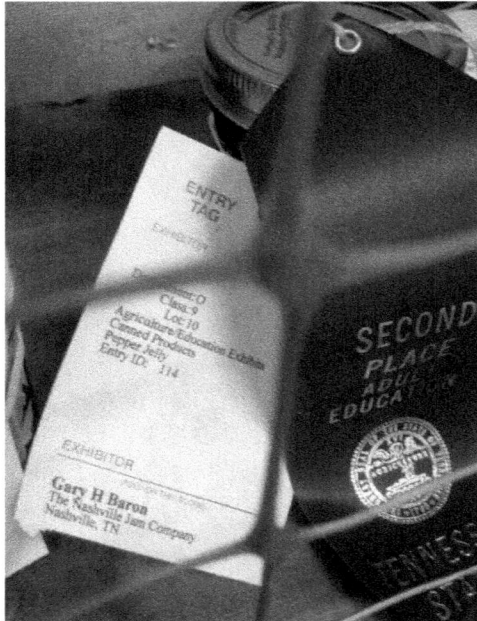

Pepper Jelly's second place ribbon at the Tennessee State Fair

Chapter 14: Ketchup
Portlandia Foods

6418 SE Foster Avenue
Portland, OR 97202
(503) 729-8257

portlandiafoods.com
jeff@pdxfoods.com

Established
2011

Leadership
Jeff Bergadine, Owner

Product
Organic ketchup under the name Portland Ketchup Company

Ketchup that's more than just a sidekick…

With his father in the Navy, Jeff Bergadine moved around quite a bit as a child. He even spent a sizeable portion of his childhood outside of the U.S. You might think someone who moved around so much might never feel comfortable in one place, but that isn't the case with Jeff. When he moved to the Pacific Northwest, it immediately resonated as home for him.

Living in Portland for the past 15 years, Jeff has no desire to live anywhere else. He has embraced the local culture and, in particular, the food scene. As a foodie himself, seeing a thriving restaurant scene with young chefs experimenting with new flavors and tastes, makes Portland a pretty exciting place to be.

He even found himself in the food industry, albeit not in the job he had envisioned for himself. He ended up in the catering business. At this point you're probably thinking, "Yeah, that is a tough road. The guy loves the food business and now he's stuck cooking rubbery chicken and other bland foods for wedding receptions and corporate gigs."

It's worse than that, though…

Jeff did end up in the catering business, but he wasn't even on the food preparation side. He was in management. So instead of a life as a respected chef in an upscale eatery, he was dealing with planning events, logistics, uninspired employees and difficult customers. Sometimes the only thing that kept him going was the dream of doing something on his own. Starting a company, doing something he loved, he could then walk away from a career he really didn't like.

Then one day it hit him. He didn't need to create some grandiose restaurant or launch a line of unusual foods. His answer as simple: ketchup.

Yes, ketchup!

It seemed to make perfect sense. Right in his hometown of Portland, he had all of these young chefs putting together these fantastic menus. There was such a degree of pride in getting the freshest ingredients and a diligent eye on getting the pairings correct it seemed ludicrous to have a dish where someone wanted ketchup and the only offering was the same bottle and same brand as you would find in a fast food restaurant or greasy spoon.

Jeff's goal was to bring ketchup up to respectability. Something that you might specifically ask for by name to enhance your meal; not something called "ketchup" which is actually a "candied tomato water" tasting concoction that you probably dump on your plate because you've been doing the exact same thing since you were three years old.

Right away, Jeff knew he could do better than the large megabrands. Their products are so loaded with preservatives, chemicals and high fructose corn syrup so they do not taste like food. They might taste like "ketchup" to the typical consumer, but that's because it's the only option they have probably been offered.

Jeff wanted his taste to come from his ingredients. Fresh ingredients without the chemicals, without the preservatives and without the high fructose corn syrup. With this goal in mind, he started developing his own brand.

His process began when he and his business partner Michael Deal took a look at each ingredient listed for the four big players in ketchup. They "deconstructed" each competitor by analyzing what each individual component on the ingredient list added to the flavor profile of the ketchup.

The top priority was to come up with what could be considered healthy ketchup. The secondary goal was to improve the flavor. Jeff and Michael felt they could do this each step of the way by analyzing the competitors and seeing if there was a healthier substitute they could utilize.

The trial and error of creating a new product is challenging. Jeff mentions how difficult it was to allow the ingredients to "do the work" for him in terms of flavoring. He laughs about initially wanting to add cayenne pepper or Allspice and thinking it was necessary to add enough to taste each specific ingredient. It was very easy to overpower flavors by making these mistakes early on.

In experimenting with recipes, there may seem to be too little of an ingredient you would think would be necessary, but at the right level it ends up playing off of the other ingredients you are adding to get the correct flavor profile.

It was these kinds of challenges Jeff and Michael were going through to develop the perfect taste. Without the finances to conduct consumer taste tests, he was regularly gathering friends and family to try his latest attempts at the perfect ketchup.

Finally, after 8 months, they had the right mixture and the Portland Ketchup Company brand was born.

One thing Jeff learned very quickly was that he wouldn't be competing against the big four on price. All of those pesticides, preservatives and fillers made for a very cheap product to bring to the market. He had a product that was well-rounded, looked great, was balanced in flavor, healthy and had great taste! This would be his approach to bring his ketchup to market.

Getting consumers to switch brands when they had been conditioned to buy certain products since they were in diapers certainly wouldn't be easy. His difficulties were compounded by the fact that he would also be charging them a higher price.

Jeff put together a pretty compelling case, though, to at least give his product a try:

Taste – By getting just the right mix of flavors, he had the perfect companion to enhance a dining experience. Just like the flavor profiles within his ketchup, his product was designed to be the perfect complement to those fresh ingredients he saw so many of those young chefs in Portland using.

Ingredients – When you look at Jeff's bottle, you know what the ingredients are. You do not need a chemical engineering degree to know what you are eating. He has found that people prefer to know what they are eating when given the opportunity to do so.

Organic – Portlandia Foods follows the governance of organic gardening so they are not utilizing any chemicals or preservatives in their product.

Healthier Option – With lower sodium, sugar and no high fructose corn syrup Portland Ketchup is a healthy alternative to the national brands.

Appearance – The competition prides itself on taste, but their taste is created with an abundance of salt and sugar. Portland Ketchup looks like food. How refreshing!

With his recipe set and list of reasons why individuals would want Portland Ketchup firmly established, he began offering it locally. When he was able to convince a restaurant to commit to his product, he found they never looked back. Customers began to ask for it by name. The restaurant owners noted customers bringing friends into the establishment to try the ketchup. These same loyal customers even approached their grocery stores to see if they sell it resulting in stores contacting Portlandia Foods about distribution.

The connection to the product never ceases to amaze Jeff. One of the favorite parts of his jobs is opening up correspondence from consumers. He speaks with great pride about the letters from families telling him how much they like his product or emails from individuals grabbing a bite after a late night and stating something like, "I can't believe I'm emailing you at 2:00 in the morning, but I just tried your ketchup and I can't believe how good it is."

There is no greater testament to the connection consumers make with his ketchup than the fact Jeff has never made a call to a wholesaler or distributor to carry his product. When a distributor gets enough calls from consumers demanding they carry Portland Ketchup, they end up calling Jeff at Portlandia Foods, and a new relationship is developed.

Recently, a few of these calls have developed into relationships with companies which have nationwide distribution. Portlandia is keeping a controlled growth approach for now, though. Opening the product up across the country too quickly could cause the company to lose sight of the important aspects which got them where they are today.

For now, Portland Ketchup can be found in Oregon, Washington, California and Idaho. The company has a website but really does not market beyond that. Word of mouth continues to be the means for them to reach new customers.

The successful launch of Portland Ketchup has Jeff and the team at Portlandia Foods looking for more opportunities as well. They have an organic mustard they are rolling out, barbecue sauces will follow and other condiments down the line. They have also experienced success in providing their ketchup in bulk sizes and doing some private label manufacturing for other companies.

While there may be headaches along the way, there are also plenty of accolades, enthusiasm and fun surrounding the successful launch of a new product, and Jeff has experienced a lot of exciting moments in launching his own brand. He also has realized the dream of leaving the catering business behind.

The ultimate experience of launching your own brand is a very simple one for him. Walking into a restaurant and seeing a bottle of Portland Ketchup on the table is a surreal moment that doesn't seem like he will ever get used to.

While there are still plenty of more dreams to chase… new products to launch, the respect of the grocery industry and perhaps even his rivals, nationwide distribution, etc., there may never be anything better than seeing that bottle on the table at a restaurant and watching someone experience his ketchup and pile the accolades on as he sits across the room.

This is something Jeff has already done many times and looks forward to doing many more. Perhaps he may even be doing it in a restaurant near you very soon!

Portlandia Foods Photo Album

Jeff Bergadine, Owner of Portlandia Foods

A bottle of Portland Ketchup

In-store product demonstration

Portland Ketchup product fact sheet

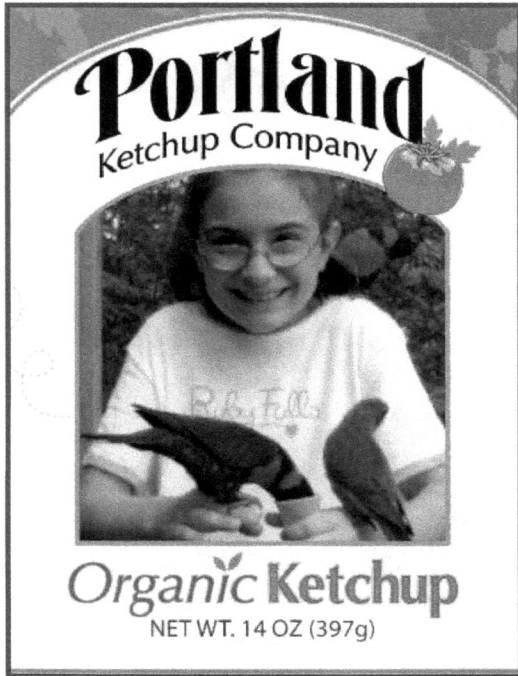

On Portlandia Food's website you can design you own label

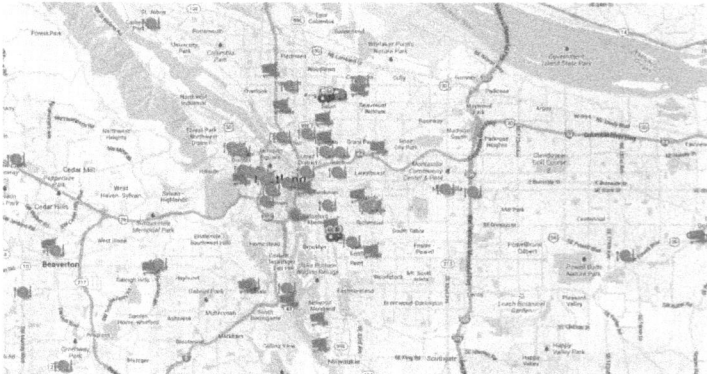

Portlandia's map is expanding quickly as ketchup sales grow

Chapter 15: Maple Syrup

Anderson's Maple Syrup, Inc.

2391 40th Street
Cumberland, WI 54829
(715) 822-8512

andersonsmaplesyrup.com
comments@andersonsmaplesyrup.com

Established
1928

Leadership
Steve Anderson President/Owner

Products
Maple syrup and maple syrup making supplies

From a family hobby to a family business...

Based in Wisconsin, today, Anderson's Maple Syrup, Inc. is the largest maple syrup company in the Midwest. Getting to this point took a little luck, a lot of work and a short diversion to Minnesota.

Paul Anderson grew up in the Cumberland, Wisconsin area which is now home to the 200+ acre farm which is Anderson's Maple Syrup, Inc. After getting married, he and his wife moved to Minnesota where he worked as a garbage man, and she cleaned houses to make ends meet. When a dairy/grain farm became available back in Cumberland, Paul jumped at the chance to get home and back to farming, something he was much more comfortable with.

During the spring offseason, Paul began to dedicate some time to making maple syrup. Initially, it wasn't a business at all. It was simply a very small operation whereby he made syrup for friends, family members and neighbors.

With the birth of his son Norman in 1928, he recognized the need for an additional revenue stream so he started Anderson's Sugar Bush to begin selling his maple syrup commercially. His time spent in Minnesota turned out to be an incredibly lucky break for someone looking to sell a retail grocery product.

One of the houses Paul's wife cleaned was owned by a high-end grocer. One call to their old friends back in Minnesota meant they had an "in" to the chain. Paul had to deliver the goods, but it was a single roundabout trip where he was able to sell all of the syrup he would produce each year to those stores.

By the early 1940's Paul's son Norman had joined his father on the farm. The two of them working together made for a team, and they started to expand their capacity and sales beyond the initial Minnesota-based chain with whom they had been working. In 1957, when it became clear Anderson's Sugar Bush was a business which could support the family, Paul and Norman sold off the dairy cows.

In 1963, Norman officially took over the company though Paul kept an active role. He continued to add parcels of acreage to expand their maple production tap on buckets. In 1973 they hit a high water mark of 18,000 tap on buckets with boiling facilities in Wisconsin and Minnesota. They ran at this level for the next 15 years until an uncle who was running the Minnesota boiling facility decided to retire.

At that point, Anderson's Sugar Bush began to take a different philosophical approach to the business.

Managing 18,000 tap on buckets is an incredibly labor intensive proposition. Now without the means to manage and process all of those taps, they had to scale back production. This was at a time when demand was continuing to grow higher and higher each year.

The company began selling equipment and educating individuals on how to cultivate maple syrup. Anderson's would then establish a buying price based on the market and buy the excess maple syrup from the individuals who purchased the equipment through them.

This ended up being a key facilitator for Anderson's to continue to experience tremendous growth in the wake of reduced ability to produce as much syrup as they had in the past. In 1993, the company was incorporated under the name Anderson's Maple Syrup, Inc. which better conveyed their role as both a producer and distributor of maple syrup and related products.

When Norman's son Steve graduated college in 1997, he took over as the president of the company. Like his father before him, Norman remains an active participant in the family business while his son runs the company.

A key component of Steve's job is managing the relationships with the individuals who sell their syrup to Anderson's. The typical producer has about 40 – 80 acres of maple trees with between 2,000 – 5,000 taps. The old "tap on bucket" systems have been replaced with sophisticated (and more tree friendly) tubes and vacuums. They typically sell about 1,000 – 2,500 gallons of syrup and deliver it to the Andersons in 30 or 55 gallon drums.

The final price is based on several factors including: color (lighter is more desirable/priced higher), taste and density. The relationships that the Anderson family have built is the backbone of their business since they currently only produce about 5% of the maple syrup they sell.

Steve Anderson notes that while the typical producer is going to be selling them from 1,000 – 5,000 gallons of syrup there really isn't any such thing as a typical producer. They are all individuals, and the amounts they sell vary widely.

He even has several individuals who sell him one gallon of syrup each season. While they may produce many more gallons than that, just like the Anderson family did when they got started, they are giving most of it to friends, family members and neighbors. There is something very appealing to the "hobby maple syrup farmer" about also being part of the well respected Anderson brand so they always save that one gallon for them. Steve treats these relationships with the same respect he does his 5,000 gallon producers. All relationships are good business.

Taking extra steps to maintain quality and consistency is one of the key differentiators between Anderson's and its competitors. Most competitors shorten the time by simply bottling the purchased syrup from their producers and getting it to market as quickly as possible.

Anderson takes an extra step which makes their syrup not only superior, but delivers the same flavor bottle after bottle for their customers. Anderson's mixes all same graded syrups into 1,500 – 2,000 gallon tanks. Rather than just bottling the syrup, they re-boil it.

Boiling syrup is something which is done in the production process and doesn't need to be repeated to sell it. By doing so, though, Anderson's gets several benefits. First of all, it "wakes up" the flavors. This brings back a freshness which gets the syrup tasting just as it did the day it was made.

Additionally, any issues with the viscosity can be worked out via a re-boil. Finally, it evens out taste. Those syrups all blend together and Steve, Norman or long-time employee Fred Buchholz can continue to blend and mix the perfect Anderson syrup by taste.

Growth for the company has come through creative marketing. A limited partnership with NASCAR® gets their company on cars or trucks for certain races. This has opened the eyes of consumers for their product as well as the doors to retailers who have also sponsored NASCAR®. Some of the largest chains they have worked their way into have come directly through this relationship.

They have even gotten creative marketing directly at the consumer level. They have an "Adopt-A-Tree" program where a customer can pay a nominal fee to adopt one of their family's maple trees. They get a certificate that contains the GPS coordinates of their tree. Several times during the year they receive emails as to what's going on with their tree in terms of maple syrup production. For those not wanting to invest in an individual tree, Anderson's runs a generic program on its Facebook® and web pages.

Despite tremendous growth and an ever-expanding reach, Anderson's closely resembles the company Paul and Norman built up so many years ago. They remain lean in terms of employees. At peak capacity, they have seven employees. They are still using the same bottling equipment as they did forty years ago. It fills eight bottles at a time with an individual starting each cap once it is full (a machine tightens them).

Each January they see interest in maple syrup production starting. In January, February and March they are selling to individuals who are actively purchasing and updating equipment. In April and May, the Anderson's are buying syrup from the producers. From June to September they are preparing, packaging syrup and working on advertising plans. In September and October syrup sales start to pick up as the weather cools leading into the peak syrup buying times of November and December.

With the internet, cooking channels and TV shows on non-food channels, foodies have more resources than ever. All of this information has created a boon of individuals seeking out high quality and nostalgic products. Anderson's fits the bill for both, and they have maintained a commitment to these attributes. Recently a trend has started where maple syrup is being packaged in flimsy plastic bags (similar to kid's single serving juices or applesauce). Anderson's refuses to jump in preferring to stick to a traditional label and packaging.

Dealing with the natural elements can make maple syrup a tough business. Getting the perfect season for maximum maple syrup production is a rarity. It blends freezing nighttime temperatures, with temps in the 40's during the day along with a mixture of snow and rain during the course of the season.

No matter what the season brings, Anderson's delivers the perfect maple syrup to its customers each and every time they buy it.

Anderson's Maple Syrup Photo Album

Paul Anderson in the Sugar House

Norman Anderson at the evaporator

Steve Anderson at the bottler

The Anderson Family

Outside Anderson's facility

Anderson's bottles

Chapter 16: Mustard
3 Monkeys Mustard, LLC

P.O. Box 6880
Lawrenceville, New Jersey 08648
(609) 577 - 2148

3monkeysmustard.com
mainmonkey@3monkeysmustard.com

Established
2010

Leadership
Dan Collins, Owner

Product
3 Monkeys Mustard

Channeling a mustard obsession into a successful business plan…

A theme which ties together many of the stories in this book is a childhood obsession which follows individuals into adulthood. At some point, these entrepreneurs act upon their personal obsessions, and their companies are born.

Dan Collin's obsession with mustard didn't occur when he was a child. When it did hit him, though, it hit him hard!

Dan's dalliance into the world of mustard started at the holidays shortly after his first son was born. He, his wife and their son were invited to a dinner party. They thought it would be appropriate to bring a small gift for the other attendees. They came up with a few ideas but ended up going with one of Dan's.

Rather than a store bought gift, he thought something homemade would be more appreciated, and it just felt more heartfelt than buying something. His idea was to create a jar of mustard for everyone. It was something they could enjoy back home after the holidays. Plus, the jars could be customized with a photo of their son.

Dan's mother made her own mustard many years before. In fact, he still had her recipe. He used it as the base for creating his own unique blend. He ended up with a mustard that yielded both flavors of sweet and spicy.

They took their six jars to the party and distributed them to their friends and family. Right away, everyone loved the photo of their son on the jar. The real delight came, though, when they tried the mustard. They absolutely loved it.

With that, a new holiday tradition was born. Each year the Collins family would bring jars of mustard to their holiday festivities. Their distribution list started to grow as word about their mustard got out within their circle of friends and family.

Soon Dan, a former finance professional turned salesman, began to add extra jars to give to clients as well. Suddenly, the Collins mustard bonanza wasn't just for the holidays anymore; Dan was producing and distributing mustard as a hobby, which started mimicking a full-time job.

He would work his regular job, then come home and devote his spare time (after his family responsibilities, of course) to making mustard. Whether it was rounding up supplies like jars, mixing ingredients or affixing labels, he acknowledges it was an obsession. Customers demanded refills, and a very successful sales career meant that Dan had an ever-growing mustard "customer" list (though he was still just distributing it on his own without any true paying customers).

As the economy reeled in 2008 and 2009, his sales numbers dramatically decreased. His company was struggling to stay afloat. Half the sales force was laid-off, and the remaining sales representatives took a pay cut.

 With the economy not looking like it was going to recover anytime soon, Dan made the tough call to end distribution of his popular homemade mustard.

Hobbies can grow tiresome, and people move on. Personal interests can change. Obsessions don't go away so easily, though.

As you can imagine, getting cutoff from a pipeline of free delicious products would upset many people. Most, while disappointed, fully understood the dollars and cents of Dan's decision.

One woman managed to stoke the passion. She literally was in tears, crying hysterically, telling Dan he didn't understand what his product meant to her. His mustard was part of her holiday traditions. She wouldn't be able to celebrate without Dan's mustard which had become part of her holiday dinners.

Seeing the personal connection someone could have to his creation really got Dan thinking about the viability of his mustard as a legitimate business. He decided to take the plunge and pursue having his mustard company as a hobby business… one he could manage in his spare time and continue to pay the bills with his regular job.

He refined the recipe to give it stabilization for a supermarket shelf. He formally named it 3 Monkeys Mustard as a tribute to his three sons he had always referred to as monkeys. He even designed his own label utilizing public domain images of monkeys. It was official; he was finally in the mustard business.

At an entrepreneurial networking and dinner event, he was approached by a graphic designer who liked his product, but told him how bad the logo/packaging looked. Dan hired him on the spot to assist with giving his product a more professional appearance.

With a great product and professional packaging, Dan felt ready to take a run at getting it on store shelves. He took it to his first store, and he was told he wasn't ready to make it on the shelf just yet. As an unknown entity, he might be better suited for a farmer's market which the store sponsored during the summer months.

Dan elected to take that route and began to set-up at the farmer's market. What happened immediately, and still does to this day, is pretty amazing: for every seven or eight people who try his product, one will buy a jar. Often, they buy more than one jar. He simply needed to get people to taste it.

After the end of the seasonal farmer's market, he did make it on the shelves of his first store, Pennington's Quality Market® in Pennington, New Jersey. Once he was in Pennington's®, it was easier to get in more. His approach remained simple: let 3 Monkeys get on the shelf, and Dan will do a demo onsite. As he had found at the farmer's market, with in-store demos he sold a jar for every seven or eight people who tried it. Surprisingly, Dan had more stores than not willing to take him up on his offer.

As a the head of a fledgling mustard empire, Dan received the ultimate confirmation he was on the right track by Barry Levenson, Curator of the National Mustard Museum in Middleton, Wisconsin. Barry and his work with the National Mustard Museum have received a lot of press for dedicating an entire museum to the history of mustard.

Dan happened to catch him on a National Public Radio® segment talking about the museum. Since he was well on his way to realizing his dream of a successful hobby business, he decided to reach out to Barry via the contact information on his website. He was pleasantly surprised when Barry returned his phone call.

Barry told him he loved his label and he wanted two jars: one to sample and one to display in the museum. Dan gladly obliged by quickly sending off the samples.

About a week later Barry called Dan back. Like a child wanting to be pumped up by the positive affirmation of a teacher or parent, Dan hung on every word when Barry started talking about his mustard. Barry stated, "Dan, I do truly love that label. I gotta tell you, though," (Dan's sweating now as Barry slowly and deliberately chose his words), "a great mustard has to be good from start to finish. You've got that! You've got a winner on your hands here!"

For a guy getting into the mustard business, this was the grand slam in the bottom of the ninth to win a World Series. Not only did Barry love the mustard, he requested Dan allow him to sell it in his online store.

As you can imagine, the National Mustard Museum has a devoted following of people who love mustard. Dan is extremely pleased to report that out of the 500+ items Barry carries, 3 Monkeys Mustard is one of the best sellers.

In 2012, Dan elected to participate in the National Mustard Day festivities at the National Mustard Museum (held yearly the first Saturday of August). He entered his mustard into the Sweet and Spicy category. He took gold for that category. After a blind taste test for all of the gold winners, he won that too. 3 Monkeys Mustard was officially the 2012 Grand Champion at the National Mustard Museum's National Mustard Day Festival!

Dan laughs about the surreal moment of beating out the big national brands. He couldn't believe he found himself autographing mustard jars and t-shirts from throngs of adoring mustard fans. It truly was the ultimate experience for someone who literally got into this business by accident.

Another big win for Dan's mustard has been local farms which have stores. He has found that not only do they do an excellent business of moving mustard for him, but also during the holidays they have a large gift basket business. Corporate clients wanting to provide gifts for customers and employees as well as individuals wanting to take a festive basket to parties are a large part of what the farms do in their nonpeak periods. Dan has found that his mustard has been a welcome addition to these baskets. It's an artisanal product, and it pairs well with the meats and cheese which are included.

Dan states he is 98% of the way to making his mustard company a full-fledged business, as opposed to the hobby business it is now. He has an ever-expanding list of stores carrying his mustard. He continues to receive accolades and awards for his product. He has repeat customers through both his farm stores and his online sales via the National Mustard Museum. He is actually have fun seeing how far he can take his company while still balancing his regular job and family life.

With the enthusiastic support of his wife, family, friends and especially his mother-in-law Linda Hoff-Woodruff (affectionately known as "Lulu"), he does see the company continuing to grow.

"Mustard Obsession," may not be yet recognized by the medical community, but it is abundantly clear Dan Collins has a pretty serious case of it!

3 Monkeys Mustard Photo Album

Dan Collins

Dan and family

Dan with his mother-in-law Lulu taking delivery of his first batch of mustard from his production contractor

3 Monkeys store demo

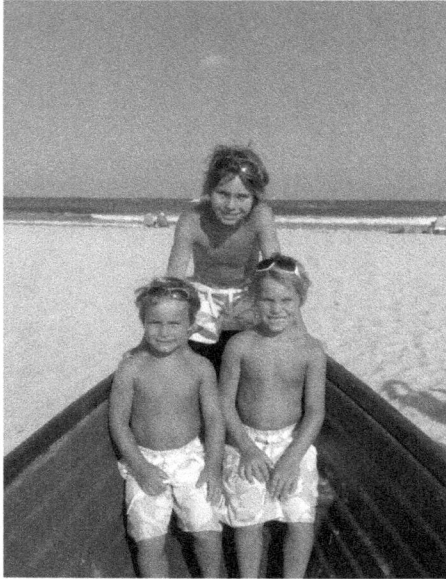

The "3 monkeys" that inspired the mustard at the beach

Compare Dan's original clipart label to his professional design

Chapter 17: Oatmeal

Umpqua Oats

UMPQUA OATS ™

6295 Harrison Drive, Suite 7
Las Vegas, NV 89120
(877) 303-8107

umpquaoats.com
info@umpquaoats.com

Established
2009

Leadership
Sheri Price, Owner
Mandy Holborow, Owner
Norm Price, Owner
Chris Holborow, Owner

Products
Single serving cups of oatmeal in the following flavors: Salted
Caramel Meltdown, Not Guilty, RU Nuts, Old School, Mostly
Sunny, Jackpot, Kick Start

The ultimate soccer moms' story…

In 1996, Bill Clinton sought reelection against both Bob Dole and Ross Perot. Election campaigns and the media, all began to pay attention to the suburban, "swing vote" mothers who were categorized as soccer moms by nature of their involvement in their children's sports. This phrase became so popular the American Dialect Society made "soccer moms" its Word of the Year in 1996 (the world chose to overlook the fact it is actually two words).

In 2008, real life Southern Oregon soccer moms Sheri Price and Mandy Holborow were actively engaged in the logistics of getting their children to their games. Breakfast on the run often meant a stop by the local coffee shop. Sheri and Mandy would often lament the lack of healthy choices at the coffee shops. The options were always limited to bread-based offerings with little nutritional value: bagels, donuts and pastries.

One day, they happily noted the addition of oatmeal to the menu. The marketing photos made the product look really good, too. It appeared to be a rolled oats-based product with fresh fruit ingredients. Finally, they thought, a healthy and delicious option had been added to the menu!

They both ordered a batch of the brand new offering. Much to their dismay, the barista simply grabbed a packet of a nationally known company's product, tore off the top, dumped it in a cup, poured hot water over it and handed it to them. Not really what they had in mind.

As they picked at the almost flavorless mush, they began to talk about how the product they were just given could be better. They discussed how fresh rolled oats could be paired with bold flavors. They also began to discuss how a business like the one they were sitting in could benefit from serving such a product. It appeared that many of the customers in the store valued the benefits of a health-conscious lifestyle. Why wouldn't they want their coffee shop to have a product that catered to them?

While a company might not have been legally incorporated at that breakfast table, all of the groundwork was worked out. They had a game plan in place to form a company they would ultimately call Umpqua Oats after the local Umpqua River.

Not ones to sit around, Sheri and Mandy immediately got to work. Initially, they were buying ingredients from the local grocery store, mixing them together and trying them out on family, friends, neighbors and even other soccer parents.

Once they had their recipes ready to go, they did some taste tests through the Food Innovation Center. The Center also was able to assist them in creating nutritional labeling information for their packaging once their testing was done and they had their recipes ready for distribution.

After establishing relationship with suppliers for their ingredients, they were able to get Sheri's kitchen FDA approved for preparing their product. Initially, Umpqua Oats was an extremely small-scale, labor-intensive operation. Sheri had her entire family assisting in the cooking of the product. Mandy was out selling. The small batches, combined with the fact every facet of the operation was run out of Sheri's home, meant that there wasn't a warehouse and inventory to pull from for orders.

In many instances, Mandy was texting Sheri as she was out in the field with specifically what she needed to fulfill an order. A meeting point was established, and someone would run her the product so she could go deliver it. They were beginning to garner some success, yet it had an odd feeling of some sort of illicit operations with texts providing instructions for parking lot meetings where checks, cash and product would be traded.

In an almost unbelievable bit of good fortune, just as they were going to market, Starbucks® was also coming out with premium oatmeal product for its stores. Initially, you may read that and wonder how the biggest player in the industry coming out with a competing product could be good news for a small company looking to bring a like product to the market.

It all stems from the fact that by nature of its footprint, Starbucks® is often a trendsetter in the industry. Once they were in the oatmeal business, other coffee shops wanted in as well. The old "rip and pour" oatmeal which Sheri and Mandy got at their coffee shop wasn't going to work, either. The coffee shops wanted a premium offering like Starbucks® was touting in its stores.

Unlike Starbucks®, most of the other coffee shops couldn't develop their own oatmeal, or get an exclusive contract for a company to create what they needed.

Enter Umpqua Oats.

They had the premium product shops were looking for in the stylish, single-serving package they needed to serve their customers. Soon Sheri and Mandy were selling their product as quick as they could make it.

They quickly moved to a 900 square foot building to create their product. That lasted four months and then they outgrew the facility. Then, they had a 4,300 square foot building for only six months until they maxed out its capacity. Finally, they secured an 18,000 square foot office, warehouse, production facility, and distribution center to meet demand.

They signed on with distributors and brokers and soon had nationwide coverage for their product. Sheri and Mandy traveled almost weekly while Sheri's husband Norm handled research and development and worked as the company's general manager. Mandy's ex-husband Chris handled purchasing and logistics.

As the company continued to expand, they began to get some interesting feedback via marketing research testing. These studies showed that their customer base was solidly in the adult 22 – 44 age range.

This wasn't grandma and grandpas' oatmeal.

Their customers were young, health-conscious consumers, just like them. Armed with this information, they looked to maximize their appeal to their demographic by redesigning their packaging to appeal to the young, hip and healthy crowd.

They switched from a traditional look to a bold package with bright colors which highlighted their ingredients by incorporating color photos designed by an artist who had actually specialized in designing skateboards.

So, what happened next?

More growth. Explosive growth. Almost unbelievable growth for a company which had just started a few short years ago.

The Umpqua team decided they needed to get a permanent home. They couldn't continue to build up, move and then repeat the process again. Plus, the wear of the frequent travel was getting to them. One of the major logistical issues facing Sheri and Mandy in their travel was the fact they needed to drive 90-minutes to get to the closest major airport.

Unfortunately, direct flights were limited so they were often then taking short flights to an international airport where they would then head to destination. Their next stop needed to be in an area with a major international airport nearby with easy access to Rancho Cucamonga, California where their manufacturing facility was domiciled.

Viva, Las Vegas!

They finally secured a location in Las Vegas where they have easy access to an airport with frequent direct flights to almost every major metropolitan area in the United States. Rancho Cucamonga is an easy 4-hour drive away as well so they seemingly have found a home where they can maximize their efficiency to continue on the fast pace they have already established.

Today, the company continues to deliver a superior product for its health-conscious consumers. Umpqua offers an all-natural product with an oats formula rolled specifically for them. Their product goes further than offering great ingredients; it represents a balanced meal. The Prices and the Holborows have worked hard to ensure their product continues to stay in touch with the demands of its buying consumer. They continue to experiment with flavors and unique ideas to grow their company.

With their growth coming so quickly, you can't simply speak about the next step; it has to be plural as in "steps." Umpqua will continue to expand in the U.S. in both the grocery and food service sectors. They are preparing to come to market with a whole new product line. International distribution is quickly approaching as well.

While it is readily apparent that the Umpqua team has been able to find a market the U.S. consumer was looking to have filled, don't downplay the hard work the creative ownership group has done to get them to this point. Their success in such a short timeframe is a testament to their vision and ability to deliver upon it. It all comes together to make for a great "only in America" story.

Even though they may represent *Small Brand America* perfectly right now, it doesn't appear that they are going to be categorized as "small" for much longer!

Umpqua Oats Photo Album

Sheri Price

Mandy Holborow

Norm Price

Chris Holborow

Example of their old "traditional" packaging

A look at their redesigned bolder packaging

Examples of Umpqua Oats point-of-sale material

Umpqua Oats product lineup

Chapter 18: Olive Oil

Hillcrest Ranch Sunol, LLC

P.O. Box 115
Sunol, CA 94586
(925) 209-7702

hillcrestrancholiveoil.com
kdell@sonic.net

Established
2008

Leadership
Kathleen D. Elliott, Owner

Products
Organic fresh extra virgin olive oil and olive oil soaps

Over 100 years in the making…

In 1913, Grace Elliott purchased a 6-acre parcel from the Thermal Fruit Company®. This spectacular property overlooked the Sunol Valley and contained olive trees, apricot trees and grapes, all sustained by six natural springs.

Kathleen Elliott was born three years after Grace, her great-aunt, passed away. Grace left the land and her home to Kathleen's father. While Kathleen never got a chance to meet her, she had a close connection to Great-Aunt Grace as her family would use the land as a weekend summer retreat from their home in San Francisco. As a young girl, Kathleen would relish these family vacations to the magical ranch where her beloved Great-Aunt Grace had once lived. As far back as her childhood, Kathleen dreamed of living there full-time, and actually turning it back into a working farm.

Kathleen was able to fulfill her childhood dream by studying agriculture and horticulture at the University of California Davis. She officially began her quest to farm the ranch in 2004 when she began pruning the olive trees so they would produce fruit. Without any pruning, the majestic olive trees which had been planted in 1890 had become overgrown. Chainsaw in hand, she began scaling back trees that encompassed a 40' x 40' area back to approximately 10' x 20' while preserving branches that flared out and down for maximum olive production. After this process was completed, it would still take four seasons for the trees to begin producing enough olives for olive oil.

In 2008 she was able to make her first harvest. This labor-intensive and time-sensitive process meant Kathleen would need to bring in 20 people to help her. In order to secure the olives without damaging them nets were placed above the ground and the branches shook and struck to release the fruit. The nets ensure the olives never hit the ground and have a soft landing preserving the integrity of her product.

As soon as her olives are harvested, Kathleen heads to the Hammer Mill. After crushing pit and all, the olives are placed in a machine called a Malaxer which slowly churns the olives' mash. Another piece of equipment called the Centrifuge/Separator takes the solids out of the mash. Finally, a Decanter/Separator takes out the water.

Kathleen utilizes a process known as "First Cold Press" since her product is directly milled right from the orchard (first) on a press without adding any heat (cold). By using the First Cold Press process, Kathleen ensures the freshest flavor for her product.

Her organic olive oil is considered Extra Virgin which is a regulated, quantitative classification which involves five chemical tests demonstrating there is no damage to the product in production as well as an additional "sensory" tests facilitated by a panel sampling the product. Extra Virgin is the highest classification with the others in descending order being: Virgin, Pure and Pumice Oil.

The final component Kathleen has which attests to the quality of her product is the fact it is unfiltered. By using the Centrifuge and Decanter Separators, combined with the First Cold Press (as opposed to a Stone Press), as well as a new stainless steel mill, she has a cleaner product that doesn't need to be filtered. A filtration not only changes the quality and taste of the product, it removes valuable and healthy antioxidants.

The final result is true "old world" olive oil with a peppery finish. Kathleen notes that a peppery finish is the mark of not only a delicious olive oil, but one that also maintains the most health benefits.

Managing the farm does keep Kathleen busy throughout the year. The olive trees need to be pruned every year so she does this on a rotational basis in January, February and March. The trees begin blooming in May. In June, olive fruit flies begin to invade.

As an organic farm, Kathleen doesn't use pesticides to manage the flies, but instead uses the traditional sticky paper traps hanging from the trees. She frequently checks and replenishes them to keep the fruit flies at bay. In November and into December, she harvests the olives. Starting in December and spilling into January, she bottles product.

In between all of this work, she is advertising and promoting her business while still working as a landscape designer, horticulturist and educator. The ranch itself is a cottage industry which goes hand-in-hand with promoting the olive business. Visitors come to visit Hillcrest Ranch to enjoy the beautiful scenery of Sunol Valley, Mount Diablo and Mission Peak.

Kathleen's property is an island in the Pleasanton Ridge East Bay Park where individuals go to hike or ride horses (she even offers a shuttle in the winter when traversing the dirt road becomes a bit arduous). They can venture up to her ranch where they can picnic or enjoy a home cooked meal from Kathleen using recipes incorporating her olive oil. Kathleen keeps walks through the orchard fun by hanging historical maps, letters and photos from the area in the trees so individuals can enjoy a history lesson as they walk the grounds.

Kathleen, a teacher by nature, also enjoys offering classes at the ranch. Individuals can learn about producing olive oil, wine tastings, agriculture/horticulture, foods made with olive oil or even how to brine olives. This popular class involves individuals picking their own olives right from her trees and preparing them with her onsite.

At the ranch Kathleen also produces her olive oil-based soaps. She produces two varieties: a lavender scented soap, using lavender grown onsite, and a gentle baby soap. Developing her soaps was a trial and error process to get the right amount of oils incorporated into her mixes. Olive oil is very moisturizing for the skin, but utilizing 100% olive oil makes for soaps without much lather, and it ends up being too soft. Incorporating coconut and palm oils gave her the right consistency and desired lather for a consumer product.

A bar of soap actually takes more than a month to produce. Her mixtures are prepared and poured into molds. After sitting to firm up, they are placed in the freezer where they can then be popped out of the molds. At this point, they still need to cure for a month at room temperature on special racks to maintain airflow.

Getting the word out about her product is often a direct connection with consumers. Whether it is through classes she offers, the open houses at the ranch, local fairs where she samples her product, or participating in contests (she is a multiple Silver winner in the California Olive Oil Council's yearly Olive Oil Competition), Kathleen maintains a lot of direct contact with potential customers in her community. Through her contacts made at these events, Kathleen has been able to get her product in many stores in the area around Sunol Valley in the San Francisco Bay area.

In addition to her teaching professionally and onsite at the ranch, Kathleen envisions expanding it beyond where she is now. She has had some discussions with the park curators about offering classes on olive harvesting in the park. Individuals could utilize the local Press and her bottling equipment to make their own olive oil.

Five of the six natural springs, which had once watered the ranch, have dried up. The apricot trees and grapes are long gone having died from a combination of old age and the fact the springs watering them are no longer flowing.

Kathleen has been blessed with continuous production from the spring which channels through to the olive trees, though. With her 120+ year old trees in infancy by olive tree standards (it's not uncommon to have trees in other parts of the world being 400 – 500 years old and it's not unheard of to have them verified at up to 3,000 years old), she has many generations of olives, and their healthy oil, to produce.

Hillcrest Ranch Photo Album

Kathleen Elliott

Handing out product samples

Looking out over the Sunol Valley

Olive tree

Olive bloom

Olives on the tree

Harvested olives

Hillcrest Ranch Products

Chapter 19: Pasta Sauce
Bove's Restaurant

BOVE'S

68 Pearl Street
Burlington, VT 05401
(802) 864-6651

boves.com
mark@boves.com

Established
1996

Leadership
Mark Bove Owner/President (affectionately known as "Head Sauceboy")

Products
Eight pasta sauces: Alfredo, Marinara, Vodka, Roasted Garlic, Basil, Roasted Tomato, and Mushroom & Wine, Three Cheese & Tomato, as well as frozen meatballs and lasagna

Kathie Lee, Hoda and Iron Chef Bobby, oh my!...

December 7, 1941.

President Franklin Roosevelt referred to it as a "date that will live in infamy" in his speech to Congress after Japan bombed Pearl Harbor.

That date also happens to be one that lives in infamy in the Bove's family history as well. Sunday, December 7, 1941, was slated to be the culmination of the dream of Mark Bove's grandparents. Their restaurant was scheduled to make its grand opening that night.

Out of respect for the military members who lost their lives, the Bove's did not open their restaurant that day. With the laws at the time limiting businesses to being opened 5-days a week, they had planned on being open Wednesday – Sunday. The Sunday grand opening would give them a chance to open to a big splash, and then retool and tweak any issues that Monday and Tuesday, before beginning a regular schedule.

Mark's grandparents reassessed their entire plans as a result of Pearl Harbor on the date of their planned opening. They ended up staying closed Sunday and Monday and having their actual first dinner service on Tuesday, December 9, 1941. From that point forward, and continuing until today, Bove's Restaurant is open Tuesday – Saturday. They remain closed on Sundays and Mondays even though the laws forbidding them to be open seven days a week have changed.

Their highly successful restaurant has been a mainstay in the Bove family ever since. While Mark had been in and around the restaurant his entire life, he officially started working there at the age of fifteen. He has witnessed the business transfer in leadership from his grandparents to his father and now to him.

The family values and core commitment to simple, fresh ingredients cooked slowly using the same old-fashioned approaches to cooking has allowed Bove's to build a solid following throughout, not only Vermont, but much of the surrounding area as well.

Under Mark's guidance, the company has flourished by staying committed to offering value for its client base. At a time when it's not uncommon to find popular Italian dishes in the $25 range, Bove's keeps its entrees priced under $10. While the traditional approach to cooking slow and making everything fresh onsite remains, Mark has expanded their sauces by adding his own sauces and recipes to the family's menu.

Grandma's marinara is still a house staple, and they diligently follow her recipe and instructions on the preparation of their flagship sauce. Mark has expanded the offerings of the company by experimenting with new flavors using the advantages of slow-cooking to create unique flavor profiles not found in mass production or prepared sauces.

Another key contribution Mark has added to the Bove's portfolio is the addition of their products being offered in-store by retailers. Growing up in Vermont, Mark has always admired the work Ben and Jerry had done to create a brand through their ice cream. He envisioned the Bove's sauces livening up dinner plates around the U.S., far outside of their home-base in Burlington, Vermont.

In 1996, he jarred his first batch of sauces and began shopping them to retailers. With Bove's being such a well-known name in the region, he was able to score some early successes by getting it on the shelves of local retailers.

When Hannaford's®, one of the largest grocery chains in New England, came calling for his sauces, the world changed in a very positive way for Mark. Because he was already on the shelves of such a large scale and respected chain, others in the Northeast quickly followed suit to get Bove's sauces in their stores.

Even with the successes he has achieved, Mark has retained the core values of Bove's family traditions. He refuses to cut corners with his products. He continues to prepare all of his products by hand, utilizing the slow-cooking methods which have worked so well in his restaurant.

He also retains a commitment to value. While the megabrands take many shortcuts to cheapen the costs of their products, Bove's looks to cut corners in company efficiencies to maintain a competitive price and value for its customers. While they may not be the cheapest, Mark works hard not to simply say, "We're a specialized product so we can be twice the cost of the name brands." He keeps a stern eye on maintaining a balance of offering a competitive price to his customers.

Currently, Mark is working hard at getting his product a bigger following west of New England. Their acceptance has been extremely positive in their backyard, but Mark wants to continue his success by finding new customers who have likely never heard of his restaurant but are looking for a brand of pasta sauce which offers a taste of what cooking was like when grandma was making a Sunday dinner.

The commitment of Mark and the Bove's family has paid off with some national exposure for the company. Bobby Flay's scout team came into Bove's Restaurant one Wednesday evening at a time when they only offered their famous lasagna on Wednesdays.

The team tried it and immediately told Mark they would be recommending Bobby feature Bove's and its lasagna on Bobby's *Throwdown! with Bobby Flay™* show. The concept of the Food Network® show is where internationally acclaimed chef Bobby Flay competes against a local dining institution by going head-to-head against their chef in preparing a version of their signature dish. Judges then select whether Bobby's version or the local chef's signature dish is better.

Bobby accepted the challenge and competed against Mark Bove on an episode of *Throwdown!™*. While Bobby Flay ultimately triumphed, Bove's was introduced to a whole new legion of fans. Mark certainly didn't take the loss too hard. Bobby Flay is one of the top chefs in the world and was incredibly gracious, and fun, during their time together making the show.

Throwdown!™ wasn't the only time the Food Network® came calling at Bove's. Melissa d'Arabian, winner of season five of the Food Network's® Show, *The Next Food Network Star™*, and host of her own show, *Ten Dollar Dinners™*, had been a student at the University of Vermont, just down the road from Bove's. The restaurant tends to be a hot spot for the college students with its affordable menu prices.

Melissa was making an appearance on the show, *The Best Thing I Ever Ate™*. The concept being self-explanatory from the title, whereby known personalities from the world of food discuss the favorite thing they have ever eaten. In Melissa's segment, she talked about Bove's Restaurant and her affinity for their signature Roasted Garlic Sauce.

Bove's was also honored to have the *Today Show*™ contact Mark about appearing on the show to make his signature lasagna dish with Kathie Lee Gifford and Hoda Kotb. For Mark, the experience was every bit as fun to do as it plays out on TV. Kathie Lee and Hoda are exactly as real and humorous as you see on the show.

Running Bove's is still a labor of love for the family. Mark enjoys working closely with his brother Rick at the restaurant. His 77-year-old father continues to come in each morning to prepare the homemade sauces.

Mark continues to not only work at keeping Bove's as popular as always, but to grow their grocery business as well. He recently added two lines to the frozen food case at the grocery store: Bove's signature lasagna and their popular meatballs.

Once again, these products are produced and sold just as they are found in the restaurant. Mark has a team of five people who only work on hand-making these new product lines for stores, and they are barely keeping up with demand.

With proven family recipes, a commitment to keep producing his products in an old-world fashion, and the boundless energy of Mark, it appears it's only a matter of time before the Bove's name is synonymous with quality pasta sauce nationwide.

Bove's Restaurant Photo Album

Mark Bove in the kitchen

The sign in front of Bove's

Mark and Chef Bobby Flay

Mark's nephew Jose enjoying some
of the Bove's family cooking

Mark making showing off his homemade
approach to his new line of frozen lasagna

Bottling sauce

Hands-on approach for every part of the business:
here's Mark stocking the shelves at a grocery store

Bove's product lineup

Chapter 20: Potato Chips
Jones Potato Chip Company

823 Bowman Street
Mansfield, OH 44903
(419) 529-9424
(800) 466-9424

joneschips.com
chips@joneschips.com

Established
1945

Leadership
Robert (Bob) G. Jones, President & Owner

Products
Jones' Potato Chips have traditional, wavy and rippled chips and come in the following flavors: Original, Salt & Vinegar, Sour Cream & Onion and Barbecue. In addition to chips, Jones also sells Potato Stix

Potato chips made by the Jones family since 1945…

Officially, Jones Potato Chip Company started operations in 1945 with Fred Jones launching a potato chip company after serving in World War II. In reality, the company roots go back a little further.

In the 1930's, and early part of the 1940's, Fred Jones owned a distribution company where he would sell consumer products like pickles, soup mixes, pretzels, nuts and cookies. One of his other product lines happened to be potato chips. When his supplier informed him they would no longer be able to supply him potato chips, he decided to simply fill the need on his own and began making chips.

With a little help in terms of knowledge from his previous supplier, Fred would take on the job of making his own chips. He began to make some inroads into getting his fledging chip company off of the ground when the United States entered World War II. With the desire to return to business after the war, Fred shut the doors on his company and enlisted in the Coast Guard.

With the conclusion of the war in 1945, Fred got out of the military and returned home to Ohio. In doing so, 1945 would become the official date of the start of the Jones Potato Chip Company (he no longer would sell other items as he had in the past).

It would turn out that the new listed date of the company wasn't just ceremonial. Fred literally had to start from scratch with his company. The contacts he had made, the relationships he built in the grocery business, all had moved on while he was away serving his country.

The initial shop was tiny. About the size of a three-car garage today. In that small location in Mansfield, Ohio, Fred began making his chips. This was a labor-intensive process in which he was kettle cooking all of the chips and packaging them for distribution. While they do not have exact numbers, his son Bob Jones, who runs the company today, estimates that Fred was likely churning out about 15 lbs. of chips an hour via his kettle system.

Of course, frying and packaging chips weren't his only jobs in running a start-up company. A good potato chip doesn't use just any potato. In fact, the potatoes we are used to seeing on our dinner plates don't work very well for potato chips. The natural sugars in them mean they turn brown when fried. While that doesn't necessarily equate to bad flavor, consumers might be put off by a chip that doesn't look like it would be delicious.

With that in mind, Fred had to develop relationships with the farmers who ultimately would provide the potatoes for his chips. While a few emails and online searches could likely provide us with that information today, it did take up a significant amount of time for Fred who was managing his relationships before the advent of the readily available information platforms of today.

As good as they were, the chips weren't going to sell themselves. After securing his potatoes, frying them up, and packaging them, his real job started, and he went out and sold the chips. As he began to make inroads in building his company, he started to hire individuals creating a yo-yo effect where Fred would bounce back-and-forth between production of the chips and selling them.

When he hired someone, it would free up his time so he could go out and focus on selling. As he built up more clients, his team back at the factory would become overwhelmed so he would head back to assisting production to meet demand. This process would continue with him hiring more workers, getting back on the street, and then starting all over again.

Seeing the limitations of his capacity, Fred got an idea to build his own fryer. His goal was to up production from the 15 lbs. per hour to somewhere between 20 and 25. His new self-engineered potato fryer far surpassed his imagination when it consistently yielded 35 lbs. an hour. This significant increase really transitioned the company from a limited operation to a company capable of meeting the demand of hungry consumers in and around the Mansfield area.

Fred's son Bob looks back with pride to the moment when his father made the leap from a limited operation to a real potato chip company. He states, "My dad liked to note that his new chip fryer didn't look good but it worked well. In fact, a competitor with many more resources heard about it. With his permission, they took a look at what he did. They were so impressed they had one built which looked way better than ours, but Dad was really pleased that not only were they interested, but that his 'uglier' homemade model worked just as well as their brand new 'beautiful' version."

As the company grew over the years, equipment upgrades allowed them to continue to meet an increasing demand. Fred's oldest son Steve (Bob's older brother) came into the business in the early 1970's, and with the two of them heading up the company, Fred witnessed his capacity grow from 15 lbs. an hour, to 35 lbs, to 350 lbs. to 750 lbs. all the way to 1,000 lbs. an hour!

Fred retired in 1986 leaving the business in the hands of Steve. In 1996, Bob Jones took over the company with Steve staying in the business until retiring in 2001. Bob has experienced his own ups-and-downs in running the family business. One of his greatest struggles came when they purchased a competitor called Thomasson's Potato Chips. The company had an extremely small, but very loyal following. Bob had hoped to capture that enthusiasm to build the brand alongside of Jones' Chips.

For 16 years they invested time and money trying to increase their strong base of followers, but it simply didn't work. Bob speaks with sadness still when he discusses the decision to close down Thomasson's. He states, "It's really difficult to discontinue an iconic brand. At the time we did it, Thomasson's had been on the market over 80 years. Nobody wants to do that. We simply couldn't make a go of it. I probably should have shut it down years before we did, but I was committed to trying to save it."

One of the company's greatest triumphs came from a phone call Bob fielded. A wholesaler contacted him desperate to fulfill orders for potato stix when their previous manufacturer suddenly went out of business. As he described his ongoing need, Bob began to think about how he could retro-fit some of his equipment to develop this new line.

"The hardest thing for me was finding out how making potato stix worked. We had the capacity. We had the connections for the potatoes, but we simply didn't know what we would have to do," states Bob. When he finally got another manufacturer to discuss it with him, he realized it would be a fairly simple conversion.

They got the necessary equipment and tried to make their first batch. Since the product cooks differently it was trial and error. Bob notes that the company used 8,000 lbs. of potatoes to create their first 100 lbs. of product as they tinkered with the settings on the equipment.

Three days later they had the product to fulfill that first order. Today, Jones' Potato Stix is a growth area for the company. Production has increased 150% in the last five years alone.

In addition to the direct benefit of the income stream of the new product line, there has also been the offshoot of new consumers discovering Jones through the Stix. It's not uncommon for consumers to contact Jones and ask if they make potato chips as well, or get on their site after enjoying the Stix and trying to find out where they can find their chips. Bob Jones states, "The way the two lines feed each other has helped us grow our business without having to increase the advertising budget and that has been a nice secondary component of adding the second line to our mix."

Currently, Jones Potato Chip Company is a 55-person operation, and the company's production now stands at 2,000 lbs of chips per hour. They utilize potato farmers in Ohio, Michigan, North Carolina, Missouri and Florida to ensure they have fresh potatoes available throughout the course of the year. The company has a large presence in the area surrounding Mansfield, and the company enjoys nationwide distribution for its products via truckload sales and in-store specials around the country.

Bob Jones is enthusiastic when he discusses the future of the company. "Currently, we are in the envious position of being only at 25% of the capacity we have available at the plant we moved into in 2009. That means we have tremendous growth potential. The really good news is that we rarely have a day go by without a phone call from a company looking for our chips or for us to manufacture a private label for them. I forecast growth in our chips, Stix and private label over the next 5 – 10 years."

For the Jones Company, and the Jones family, making potato chips remains a family tradition. Since the Jones children have been old enough to join the family business, there have continually been between 6 and 9 family members working for the company at any given time. Bob notes the leadership has always been a family member, and they have been able to carry on the family business without the in-fighting or difficulty of leadership transition other small companies have witnessed.

As they close in on their 70th year in business (or perhaps 80th if you count Fred Jones' time in the chip business before World War II), the Jones family looks forward to you finding their chips at a store near you!

Jones Potato Chip Company Photo Album

Fred Jones in the late 1960's

The original Jones' Potato Chip delivery truck

Jones' Potato Chips bag label

Potato Chips production line

Jones' Potato Stix label

Potato Stix on the scale

Chapter 21: Pudding (British)
Sticky Toffee Pudding Company

1313 West 9½ Street
Austin, TX 78703

stickytoffeepuddingcompany.com
tracyclaros@stickytoffeepuddingcompany.com

Established
2004

Leadership
Tracy Claros, Founder

Products
Five British puddings (Sticky Toffee, Hot Chocolate Fudge Cake, Tart Lemon Pudding, Molten Chocolate Baby-Cake and Sticky Ginger Pudding), three "Sticky Bars," a seasonal Plum Pudding and a seasonal Brandy Butter

A little bit of indulgence from the other side of the pond…

Moving around frequently as a child, a constant in Tracy Claros' life was her love for baking. She was born in England, but also lived in Germany, Brunei, Cypress and the Isle of Man to name a few of the places she lived. No matter where they were, there was always one constant: Saturdays were baking days where she and her mum would bake fresh goods.

Her obsession with baking wasn't just limited to the Saturday morning sessions. While other preschoolers might enjoy reading the likes of *Clifford the Big Red Dog*™, Tracy preferred thumbing through Mum's *Good Housekeeping*™ cookbooks. The list of ingredients and black-and-white photos of the completed dishes fascinated her.

She also had another unique manifestation from her love for baking: an uncanny ability to remember exactly what everyone ordered during a stop at a bakery. Initially, that might not sound too unusual. But for a toddler, being able to run back through an entire order from a bakery the family had stopped at a week before, was actually a pretty good parlor trick. She could go person-by-person for everyone in their group and know exactly who ordered éclairs, who had Napoleons, who had the sticky toffee pudding, etc.

While in boarding school living on the Isle of Man, her best friend was a Nigerian national. After graduation, she went to visit her friend at her home in Nigeria. While there she met a Bolivian man working on his PhD. He was doing some grant work while working on his education for the University of Texas – Austin. They began dating during her stay in Nigeria.

Now in love, Tracy followed him to the United States to live in Austin, Texas. They ended up getting married, and Tracy also went back to school and completed her undergraduate and graduate work in communications.

She then began to work as a speech therapist in the Austin area. Her marriage ultimately ended in divorce so she decided to leave the United States.

Always the world traveler, she was free to go anywhere there was an opportunity to use her skills as a speech therapist. She ended up finding a job in Ghana, Africa. After spending some time there, she decided it would be good to get back to her original home of England. While living back home in England she noticed that chefs were getting very creative with the traditional English dessert of sticky toffee pudding.

She began to think about her time in the United States and how she had never even seen anyone offering this favorite British dessert while she lived there. In fact, British desserts and U.S. desserts seemed to be different altogether. In England, fresh cakes and puddings ruled. In the U.S. there was a greater focus on packaged or frozen desserts.

While she had always loved baking, she never wanted to just try her version of a popular dish. She wanted to be groundbreaking and totally different if she were ever to get into the baking industry. She began to see the U.S. as an untapped market to introduce sticky toffee pudding. This unique opportunity would allow her to bring innovation to a new product and market, while hedging her bet with something she knew was extremely popular in her home country.

With no real self-employed business experience, she took a chance and headed back to the United States. In doing so, she headed to the city she knew best, Austin.

The baking portion of the equation was not a problem. Tracy had a lifetime of experience producing unbelievably tasty treats. Her issue was the business side, but initially, "when you don't know what you don't know," it wasn't a problem.
She baked some of what would become her flagship item, sticky toffee pudding, and took them to the local farmer's market. She quickly sold through her stock.

After continued success at the farmer's market, she decided to test the waters with selling them in some of the local grocery stores. Her first visit was to Whole Foods®. A friend, seeing her naiveté in dealing with the likes of big business versus single consumer at the farmer's market, asked her what she was going to do about cash flow.

"Cash flow?" Tracy retorted, "Why would that be an issue? I'm selling my product, so I'll have money coming in."

Tracy was able to comply with everything Whole Foods® needed to get her product on the shelves, and she was handed the largest single order she had gotten to that point. It seemed like life couldn't get any better.

It was about to, though.

The stores sold out instantly. Those sticky toffee puddings flew off the shelves.

That's what every entrepreneur wants, right?

The problem was the store manager called her in a panic. Double the orders and get them here right away!

Tracy had spent all of her money putting together her first order and now she wasn't going to be paid for weeks. While she had happen what every person staring their own business wants to occur, it had created its own unique set of problems. The issue of "cash flow" had in fact gotten her!

Through some creative financing, Tracy was able to fulfill her second order, but she did learn some valuable business lessons along the way. Managing cash flow is something which has become a regular part of her job as the owner of a small company.

Looking at when she can purchase the unique packaging she utilizes from Denmark, for instance, becomes a balancing act based on when she will be getting paid from customers. The "logistics of cash" is a huge issue for the small companies trying to battle it out versus the megabrands.

Wanting to expand her product line to make it more appealing for stores looking for a family of products has also been a key initiative for Tracy. She has refined her British puddings to add more flavors, and currently has five she is selling. In addition, she has recently added a line of bars inspired by the flavors she found living in different parts of the globe. She also imports a Christmas pudding, specially formulated for her company, from England during the holidays and a brandy butter to go with it.

One of her biggest challenges for success has been the fact her dessert is so unique in America; it doesn't fit the system of categorizing items for buyers. Is it a pudding? Is it a chilled dessert? Is it a cake? As such, it can be difficult for her to get some of the larger companies onboard with the idea of offering sticky toffee pudding to its customers.

Another highlight for Tracy has been her relationship with Costco®. That relationship has brought her all the way from a local/regional supplier to a global dessert company. During last year's holiday season, Costco® committed to buying 10,000 units for their stores in western Canada. They ended up buying 20,000!

Her desserts have been so popular Costco® is now looking to introduce them to their stores in the Pacific Rim. Recently, Tracy has been busy sending samples to stores in Japan, Korea and Taiwan. The possibilities seem endless at this point.

The best part of Tracy's situation is she has managed to avoid what so many entrepreneurs tend to do when they begin to experience success. Despite offers, and the appeal of a cash infusion, Tracy has steadfastly declined investments in her company. By doing so, she has retained 100% of her business which allows her to control the quality of her product and growth of her company.

She has also learned well the lessons of cash flow. She has been able to maintain a business with no long-term debt.

In addition to exceeding sales expectations, Sticky Toffee Company's products continue to impress the industry as well. Tracy is a three-time Gold Medal winner at the prestigious food competition at the Fancy Foods trade show in New York.

If Tracy continues on the trajectory she has been, it's safe to say that sticky toffee pudding won't be just the favorite treat of Great Britain. It's looking more and more like she is finding a global affinity for her hometown favorite.

Just like Mum used to make!

Sticky Toffee Pudding Company Photo Album

Tracy Claros

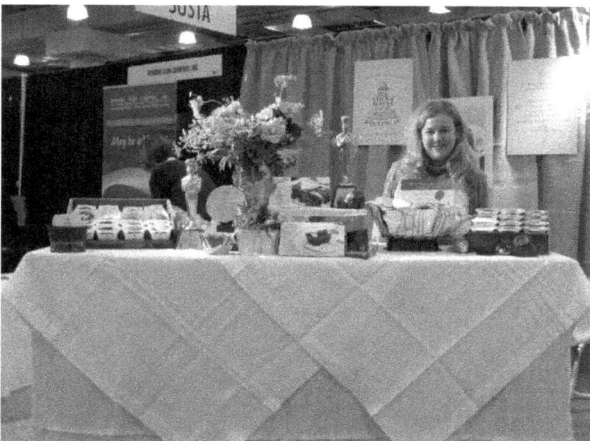

Tracy at a food show in New York

Tracy collecting an award for one of her outstanding desserts

Tracy preparing some chocolate

The famous sticky toffee pudding

Tart lemon pudding

Tracy's newest offering is sticky toffee bars in the following flavors:
- Millionaire Shortbread with Smoked Hickory Sea Salt
- Chocolate Tiffin with Biscuits, Roasted Almonds and
- Cherries and Toffee Flapjack and Sesame

A look at the Sticky Toffee Pudding Company's packaging for its sticky toffee pudding lineup

Chapter 22: Salad Dressing

Jimmy's Salad Dressing & Dips

1711 2nd Avenue NW
Stewartville, MN 55976
(507) 533-7786

jimmysdressing.com

Established
1973

Leadership
Tom Slightam, Owner/President

Products
Salad dressing, dips, tartar sauce and salsa (22 products in total)

Homemade taste and hometown goodness…

In 1958, drive-in restaurant owners Jimmy Slightam and his wife Ella decided to purchase The Fish House, a local restaurant which had been in business since the 1930's. The rationale being a sit-down restaurant offered consistent income versus the drive-in which was a seasonal business.

Jimmy brought his own touches to the restaurant by revamping some of the menu items. Some of these changes included offering homemade versions of the salad dressings and the house tartar sauce.

His signature salad dressing was an innovative take on 1000 Island. In his recipe he didn't use pickle relish, but instead substituted onion and garlic. Customers loved it. In fact, there soon came a strong demand from customers to make it available for them to take home.

Running a restaurant doesn't leave a whole lot of time for side projects, but by the mid-1960's Jimmy knew he had to acquiesce and get his dressing in grocery stores for his loyal customers.

With that, he launched a line of four dressings under The Fish House name: 1000 Island, Blue Cheese, French and Tartar Sauce. The demand was so high, and the name so well known in the area, Jimmy was able to secure a high percentage of distribution in a 50-mile radius surrounding Stewartville, Minnesota where the restaurant was located.

As a child growing up with a family-owned restaurant, Jimmy's son Tom came into the business at a young age. By 10 he was coming into help out by doing odd jobs. At 15, he had a regular job at the restaurant working 3-days a week.

Tom continued to work at the restaurant through high school. In 1982, he rented out the basement of The Fish House and opened his own tavern.

By the late '80's, Tom had grown tired of the rigors of owning a tavern. His parents were starting to slow down and ponder retirement. Tom felt it was a time to take a look at the salad dressing business and assess whether it was going to continue after his father retired.

While it never really took off, The Fish House dressing did represent a steady stream of income with little attention being paid to it. Tom believed with the proper focus there was the potential to really grow the business beyond what his father had done.

In 1990 he purchased The Fish House dressing from his father. He began to take a look at getting the product in stores beyond the 50-mile radius where they already had a strong presence. He kept running into the same problem again-and-again, though. Outside of the area where individuals knew The Fish House restaurant, the name was a hindrance.

What was The Fish House dressing?

Did it smell or taste like fish?

Were these toppings for fish dishes?

Tom's first major decision as owner of his father's dressing company was to change the name. He had the perfect plan. He would call them Jimmy's as a tribute to his dad. After all, he had created the recipes.

Armed with an idea for the new name, he presented it to his father. Was he thrilled that his salad dressing and tartar sauce would now bear his name?

Nope.

Dad wasn't happy with the idea of changing the names of his dressings. He had built the name and reputation of The Fish House for over 30 years. He didn't like the idea of changing the name, nor did he like the idea of it being named after him. Despite his father's resistance, Tom forged ahead with the name change.

Tom's idea to get the product to market was to simply go out and hustle. He needed to get it in front of as many potential buyers as possible. He couldn't turn this over to anyone else, either. He had to be the person going in and talking to potential customers about the merits of his products.

Tom was an early adopter of consultative selling as well. With each produce manager he met (Jimmy's is a fresh/refrigerated product so it is sold in the Produce Department), Tom would spend some time asking about what products they could use in their store which they currently didn't have.

During these sessions, he kept hearing about the need for a vegetable dip. They might be interested in the dressing, but if they had a vegetable dip, he'd be in for sure.

Tom took this knowledge back to his father. Jimmy was a master in pairing flavors and creating these unbelievable profiles just by tasting and experimenting. Tom knew he would need his buy-in if he was going to launch a new product line.

He told his dad about all of the conversations and how many buyers stated they were looking for a vegetable dip. Jimmy flat out told him it wouldn't sell. Tom convinced his dad to at least try to put something together for him.

While his dad was experimenting with the vegetable dip recipe (under protest), Tom went out to find someone to print plastic containers for the new product he hoped to be adding to the mix.

A few days later his dad handed him a bowl of dip and stated, "Here you go, this is what I came up with for you." Tom tried it and couldn't believe it. The flavor of that dip just jumped out of the bowl.

Tom immediately said, "Dad, did you write the recipe down. This is perfect. We won't change a thing."

Luckily, Jimmy did write it down, so Tom was now in the Vegetable Dip business. He called his container guy and placed the order. Admittedly, he couldn't believe the minimum order he had to place to be able to get the bowls printed.

When they arrived, his dad went through the roof. They had bowls stacked floor to ceiling anywhere there was a flat spot. His dad presented him with a quick calculation which showed it would take him over 10 years to work through the inventory of Vegetable Dip containers he had ordered.

Three months later they filled the last container of the original order, and Jimmy never questioned Tom again. He happily assumed the role of product development!

With Tom working the stores, and Jimmy working on new flavors, they managed to expand the company quickly from a local provider to a regional brand.

While Jimmy is now retired, he continues to come in each morning at 6:00 a.m. for coffee. The company now has 22 total products including: 12 salad dressings, a tartar sauce, 3 fruit dips, 5 vegetable dips and a salsa. Most of Jimmy's products still feature his original recipes. Future ideas include focusing on developing additional healthy product lines.

Currently, Jimmy's is widely available in Minnesota, Wisconsin and Iowa. The company hopes to expand beyond being a regional player by showcasing its coleslaw dressing line which is proving to be popular with barbecue. Currently, the coleslaw line offers an original, a fat-free and a pineapple.

Participating in barbecue festivals has introduced Jimmy's to a brand new audience. This enthusiasm from the barbecue community has opened doors for the company, and they hope to continue to expand their reach utilizing the coleslaw line.

Tom Slightam is quick to point out that a focus on quality and a small, but dedicated group of employees is a major component of their success. He notes many of his long-term employees share the same dedication to the brand as he does.

It doesn't matter if they were mixing salad dressing in 25 gallon containers with a canoe paddle like they used to, or in a modern facility as they do today, Jimmy's remains committed to offering a superior product with the freshest ingredients, nothing artificial and no preservatives.

When you can sell a 10-year supply of Vegetable Dip containers in three months, you know it has to be good!

Jimmy's Salad Dressing & Dips Photo Album

Jimmy at the Drive-In in 1956

Artist's rendition of what The Fish House looked like in 1960

Ella and Jimmy Slightam in 1980

Jimmy and Tom Slightam in 2012

The original label with The Fish House logo

CELEBRITY Status

By Rebecca Youngman

Sisters Lola Wendt and Florence Yeadon help put Jimmy's Dressings and Dips on the map!

Florence (left) and Lola (right) are standing with the founder of Jimmy's Salad Dressings and Dip, Jimmy Stigman.

Jimmy with sisters Lola Wendt and Florence Yeadon. The sisters were long-term employees that worked at both the restaurant and the salad dressing/dip company. They gained local celebrity status by appearing in TV ads for Jimmy's.

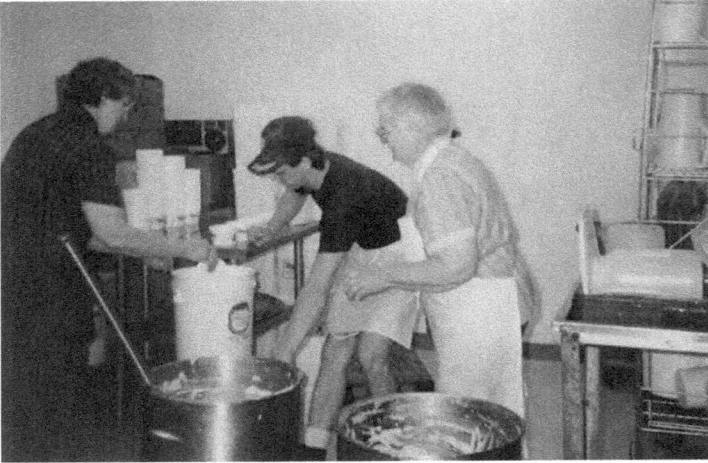

Mixing up dressing in 1989

Three generations of Slightams: Griff, Jimmy, Tom & Sam

Chapter 23: Seafood

CBS Foods, Inc.

2020 Fieldstone Parkway, Suite 900-179
Franklin, TN 37069
(800) 216-9605

chefbigshake.com
info@chefbigshake.com

Established
2007

Leadership
Shawn Davis, Founder and CEO

Products
The Original Shrimp Burger, Cajun Shrimp Burger, Chesapeake Bay Shrimp Burger, Jalapeno Shrimp Burger, Teriyaki Shrimp Burger, Veggie Burger, Lobster Pot Pie, Lobster Mac and Cheese, Cajun Shrimp Nuggets, Cajun Popcorn Shrimp and Chef Big Shake's Finger Lickin' Hot Sauce

Shakin' up the seafood industry…

Shawn "Chef Big Shake" Davis, a Bayshore, New York native, was a bit rambunctious as a preteen. Rambunctious is a nice way to say he got into trouble… a lot of trouble! Nothing terrible, mind you, just enough to make life difficult for himself and to cause his mother to search for answers.

When he was twelve and preparing to get out of school for the summer, his mother became worried about what sort of problems Shawn might encounter with so much time on his hands. When a friend told her about a restaurant looking for a dishwasher for peak season on the popular New York tourist area of Fire Island, she inquired and was able to get Shawn the job. Doing so meant he would take the ferry and stay with the restaurant owner's family for the summer.

At only twelve years of age, Shawn was terrified to say the least. That began to change when he got to Fire Island and found a welcoming environment filled with structure which gave him the discipline his mother was seeking for him. He liked it so much he continued to go back year-after-year with increasing responsibilities each season.

After his year as a dishwasher, he spent the next summer as a prep cook. The year after that he became a line cook. It was his first year as a line cook where he got the nickname of "Chef Big Shake." Only 14, he was stepping up to a role few early teens fulfill. A big kid, he looked the part, but he was nervous just starting out so he was actually shaking. Someone referred to him as Chef Big Shake, and the name stuck.

By age 16 he was the head chef at the restaurant. His passion for food and creative cooking was established. He continued to work at the restaurant during his years in college at Norfolk State University. While at Norfolk, he studied hotel and restaurant management. It was during his time there that he would first experience the entrepreneurial spirit that would later define him as a person.

Chef Big Shake went to work with a small dinner business which he ran out of his dorm room. He would make Caribbean food each afternoon, starting at about 3:00 p.m. He would then package it so it would be a simple carryout dinner for his fellow students. By 5:00 p.m. each day, his fellow hungry students had him sold out. With just two hours of work each day, he was able to cover his college bills and have some spending money while he was at school.

His cooking skills also were able to do more for him than just put money in his pocket. Shawn proudly discusses how he was able to win the heart of his wife Robin with his cooking. He states, "The first time I cooked for her, I knew I had her!"

In the early 90's Shawn feels the landscape of the restaurant business was far different than it is today. With TV and local chefs garnering so much respect, the profession seems like a strong career path. At the time he was graduating, Shawn believes working in the restaurant business often had the negative connotation that those jobs were more for individuals who couldn't find work.

Wanting to rise above where he came from, Shawn didn't pursue work in the food industry, even though it was what he knew best. Instead he went to work for corporate America. Shawn went to work for G.E. Capital® where he experienced success in the corporate world holding several positions.

The pay was good, the benefits were solid and he was working for a respected company. As a self-explained "serial entrepreneur," Shawn always had other start-up companies he was doing on the side while working at G.E. He had painting and carpet cleaning companies. He even continued to rely on his culinary background by offering cooking classes, catering or finding work as a personal chef.

The game changer for him came about one day when his daughter came home from school and declared she was no longer going to eat meat. Shawn convinced her she needed protein so she should at least continue to eat seafood.

Using his Chef Big Shake skills, Shawn began to get creative with dinners so his daughter could enjoy a variety of healthy food choices while maintaining her new vegetarian lifestyle.

One night the family was having a burger night. Not wanting his daughter to miss out, Shawn created what would become known as his Original Shrimp Burger. It was so good, Shawn, along with his wife and son, agreed that his daughter's shrimp burger was better than their hamburgers.

The family continued to enjoy the shrimp burgers and soon began to talk about them with friends and extended family. When they sampled the shrimp burger they too gave it rave reviews. Shawn knew he might have something special.

He took samples to restaurants and couldn't believe it when they began ordering his shrimp burgers. Soon, he was offering his Original Shrimp Burger to grocery stores. He envisioned a seafood company which offered restaurant quality food and packaging with an affordable family-friendly price. Little did he know, the opportunity was about to find him.

Initially, he continued to work at G.E.® as he pursued his "Plan B," selling the Original Shrimp Burger full-time. As the business continued to blossom, he ultimately left the company but had to continue to work multiple jobs to make ends meet for his family. Working as a personal chef and catering gigs became a necessary evil for him to continue to pursue his dream of running his own seafood company, even if he really didn't have time to do those things. He simply was going to achieve his goals by out-working others.

A friend of the family was a fan of the show Shark Tank™. He filled out an application for Shawn and his Chef Big Shake Original Shrimp Burgers to be on the show. Shawn was taken completely by surprise when a producer called him to be on the show. They were interested in his product and asked him to come to California to meet regarding making an appearance on Shark Tank™. Utilizing the same "elevator speech" he had already used a million times, he passed the litmus test and received an invitation to a taping.

With that, Shawn was going to be pitching his product to five billionaire potential investors, or sharks, to see if they wanted to invest in him and his company. While you wish every story had the perfect ending, Shawn's time "in the tank" was extremely entertaining TV, but he left without a deal. It seemed like the group genuinely liked him and the product, but they weren't a good fit for bringing a frozen seafood line to the market.

Knowing that five people, any of which could have immediately given him the credibility he needed to get on store shelves nationwide, had passed on an investment opportunity for the Original Shrimp Burger, and his dream, was tough. The six months between the show being filmed and airing was a time of great self-reflection for Shawn. He knew that despite the fact he didn't "get a deal," he was going to continue on his own with Chef Big Shake's Original Shrimp Burger.

Then the show aired.

As soon as it did, his dreams began to come true. The next day his email and phone were filled with messages of well-wishers and investors. He had to spend some time combing through the opportunities (some were people legitimately with money but they apparently wanted to play the "at-home game" of Shark Tank™ by trying to negotiate a percentage of his company over the phone). When it was all said and done, he had two partnerships which would begin to make Chef Big Shake a household name. He had an investor who offered more than money; he was a true partner helping him out in growing his business. He also was able to secure a relationship with a brokerage company specializing in seafood distribution. They had the contacts to get his product to market.

Business couldn't be going better for Chef Big Shake. He now has a quickly expanding line of seafood products and has accomplished just what he always wanted: affordable prices with restaurant quality. Mark Cuban, one of the sharks who passed on working with him, has given him some great business advice to help grow his company. Mark has even noted in multiple TV interviews that his biggest regret from Shark Tank™ was not investing in Chef Big Shake.

Shawn continues to be the same humble person as the kid shaking while working the line at the restaurant on Fire Island. He takes a hands-on approach to his rapidly growing business. A typical day has him starting at 5:00 a.m. answering emails. He then checks on the deliveries from the day before to ensure they made it on time. He checks on production to find out exactly what is being made that day. Then he checks with his broker to see where they are on inventory.

As the face of the brand, he is also in high demand with the media. Two to three times a week he is doing interviews, promotions or in-store demos. In the fall of 2013 he is doing a nationwide Shrimp Burger Tour to promote his brand. He will be on hand at stores in cities around the country personally handing out samples.

Shawn Davis never forgets that everything he has accomplished all started with his mother looking for answers for a troubled child. He continues to give back by speaking at schools and youth groups telling his inspiring story and encouraging the kids to follow their dreams as he did. He often notes you may not find your calling right away, but keep trying. After all, it took Chef Big Shake's diversions in the corporate world, a painting business and a carpet cleaning company to find what he was destined to do.

With the passion, boundless drive and energy of Shawn Davis, there is little doubt the Chef Big Shake brand name is about to become as well known as the megabrands he is currently competing against.

CBS Food, Inc. Photo Album

Shawn "Chef Big Shake" Davis

Shawn at home with his family

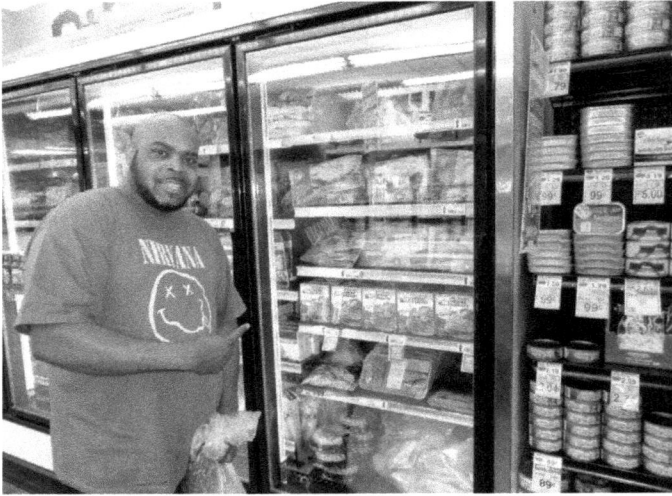

Chef Big Shake checking out his products at a store

Chef Big Shake's product line now includes
items like Lobster Mac & Cheese

The Original Shrimp Burger

Packaging for Chef Big Shake's flagship item

Chef Big Shake has started offering new Shrimp Burgers to the line like this example of his Chesapeake Bay Shrimp Burger

Shawn Davis' dream of offering restaurant quality seafood for budget conscious consumers seems to be coming true with examples like this Lobster Pot Pie he is now offering

Chapter 24: Soda

Jackson Hole Soda Company

1112 Oakridge Drive, Suite 104-299
Fort Collins, CO 80525
(307) 920 - 0018

jacksonholesoda.com
bill@jacksonholesoda.com

Established
2010

Leadership
Bill Leary, President

Products
Old fashioned sodas in the following flavors: High Mountain Huckleberry, Snake River Sarsaparilla, Buckin' Rootbeer, South Fork Strawberry Rhubarb, Outlaw Orange Cream, Jackson Ginger and Grand Teton Grape

The best dang old fashioned soda in the whole darn country…

The goal of any entrepreneur is usually pretty simple: to grow his or her product.

The truth is, success can cause its own unique set of problems. An unexpected upward trajectory in sales can often leave a small business in dire straits as they look to meet demand on a level they hadn't anticipated so soon.

Whether it's the inability to produce enough product due to capacity constraints, quality issues, or cash flow problems, unchecked growth can be as equally detrimental as a lack of sales.

Jackson Hole Soda experienced this very issue. Rapid growth caused the company to teeter on the verge of extinction before a new sheriff came to town to clean up the mess.

Initially, Jackson Hole Soda was an early success. Based out of its namesake Jackson Hole, Wyoming, the company instantly connected with consumers who were looking for something that was not only different, but utilized the natural sweeteners of cane sugar as opposed to the high fructose corn syrups the mega national brands utilized.

Jackson Hole fit the bill on both fronts. The soda not only used the old fashioned sweetener of cane sugar, it had a unique look with its retro Wild West theme, and they had a variety of unique flavors.

As Jackson Hole Soda began to grow, it looked like it was a bona fide hit. Sales growth meant that the company was outgrowing its Jackson Hole production and distribution facility. A move was warranted so the company owner sought a new, larger production plant.

When a deal on a manufacturing and distribution facility in Colorado became available, it was too good to pass up. Jackson Hole Soda was about to become a Colorado-made product. Seemingly, the good fortune continued after the move. The soda caught on so quickly, it soon became apparent the new Fort Collins facility wasn't going to be large enough to meet demand.

This upward growth meant an already cash-strapped owner had to begin looking for creative ways to meet demand since the company was locked in at the current location for the near future.

His solution was to begin to piecemeal out portions of the production. No longer could they make all flavors in-house, so the company began to utilize different vendors to facilitate runs of Jackson Hole's sodas.

Consistency of production and the overall quality of the product began to suffer. Once this happened, sales began to drop. Now began the slippery slope of an all out downward spiral.

Jackson Hole Soda had managed to fall even quicker than it rose.

At the same time, Bill Leary was in year twelve of what seemed like a lifetime sentence in the insurance industry. He was burned out and ready to make a change.

Out of the blue, a friend called him and told him about Jackson Hole Soda, and the fact it might be for sale. While Bill always liked soda and loved the idea of working for himself in a business his family owned, he had to pass. Neither he, nor the family, knew anything about the soda industry or had any experience in manufacturing.

As he got back to serving his insurance sentence, the thought of running a soda company continued to linger. Soon, he had a change of heart, and it was decided he and his family would pursue the Jackson Hole Soda company. In 2010 he was officially paroled from the insurance industry, and he was now a soda baron.

His first order of business was to get rid of all inventory on-hand. The quality of the product was unknown and going to market with it might mean he was continuing the downward spiral.

Once he had his arms wrapped around the overall operation, he looked to production facilities which could meet his strict standards and produce the soda for him.

He sought to outsource production to a facility capable of meeting his needs now but also having the ability to increase production as the business started to grow again. After a long search, he was able to find a warehouse and production plant in California. They would allow him to formulate the recipes, order the raw materials and ship it to them and then follow his precise instructions on producing the actual soda. It was the perfect situation and allowed him to avoid the pitfalls he had seen the previous owner make.

With the issue of production behind him, Bill was able to focus on managing distribution channels and inventory.

Managing distribution channels is a big job because it involves dealing with distributors and securing direct orders. Bill has found that the key to selling his product to buyers is as follows in order of importance:

1). Flavor – His flavors have to be unique and stand out above competitors.

2). Look – Customers are initially attracted to the product by its packaging. Jackson Hole's bottles look like you are quenching your thirst in 1880. This fun look has proven to be popular with consumers.

3). Can they sell it? – Is Bill's product right in that sweet spot of great and unique flavors, excellent packaging and the right price point?

When he hits on all three of those at once, he has a new customer.

His other big job is managing inventory. It's a much bigger undertaking than you might initially think. He has to stay on top of how much of each type of soda he has on-hand versus what is coming up in terms of orders. Getting more of any of his flavors involves ordering raw materials and coordinating everything with the production team in California. It's not something you can do in a few days so he always has to be anticipating where he is with his inventory.

Jackson Hole Soda can be found in over 30 states. By far his most popular offering is his High Mountain Huckleberry. Fans of this berry found in the mountainous areas of the Pacific Northwest enjoy his spot-on tribute to their favorite fruit. The taste is so revered Bill has heard from many people who take a bottle to their local snow cone stand and just get plain ice and pour it right over their snow cone.

He does note there are pockets where each of the individual flavors are appreciated. For example his Snake River Sarsaparilla happens to outsell the rest of his offerings in the Northeast.

Currently, Bill is researching the idea of adding a lemonade and limeade to his business mix. Just like Jackson Hole Soda, these fruit juices under the brand name Key West would be sweetened with cane sugar. His product formulations and production are ready to go, but he is approaching this new adventure slowly. With a whole new set of distribution channels, and the fact it is a perishable product, he wants to be sure everything is in order before he green lights this new product line.

The goal for him is to continue to grow the company. He has young children, but he could envision himself continuing to work on the brand until his kids are ready to enter the business.

The profit margins in the soda business may be thin (as low as $2.00 a case), but Bill Leary has found a way to build Jackson Hole's sales back up and to make money on volume. With his dedication to a quality product, combined with the flexibility to grow, it looks like Jackson Hole is only heading upward now.

Each time Bill takes a swig of one of his own products, he gets a good laugh from how much fun he is having at what he's doing. People look forward to meeting him and being introduced to his product, unlike those long days when he was selling insurance and his customers were just as miserable listening to his sales pitches as he was selling it.

While Jackson Hole Soda celebrates years gone by, the real celebration for the company is a bright future under the guidance of Bill and his team!

Jackson Hole Soda Company Photo Album

Bill Leary

Bill's other passion: his family

The company started out in Jackson Hole, Wyoming…

…but later moved to Colorado

Even working a tradeshow is a family affair

Jackson Hole Soda Company product lineup

A look at Jackson Hole's fun labels

Chapter 25: Teriyaki
Mr. G's Hawaii-Style Teriyaki

Reno, NV
(775) 846-1829

mrgsteriyaki.com
george@mrgsteriyaki.com

Established
2008

Leadership
George and Susie Kapahee, Owners

Products
Hawaii-style teriyakis in the following flavors: Spicy Garlic, Hot Spicy Garlic, Ginger Wasabiyaki, Red Hibiscus and Pineapple, Mango, Poke, Tangerine, Pineapple Plum and a Thai Pepper barbecue sauce

From the Kapahee ohana to your ohana…

George Kapahee grew up on the island of Maui in Hawaii. Far removed from the tourist-side of the island, he was raised in a rural setting under the wing of Lucy Lani, his grandmother and the matriarch of the ohana (Hawaiian for family).

Lucy was of full-blooded Hawaiian descent, and she always stressed the importance of family, celebrating and cooking with the traditional Hawaiian foods (like fresh fruits, sea salts and fresh spices like ginger).

After following his sister to the U.S. mainland to go to college, George decided to stay. He eventually settled in Reno, Nevada. It was there, he met Susie, a Reno native, while they were both working at a local bank.

George and Susie fell in love and were married. Eventually, they would have two children together. They didn't stay at the bank, though. Susie went to work for the county, and George worked at a golf course and then started his own lawn care company.

When their children were grown and Susie at retirement age from the county, they began to explore something new to challenge them. One thing which immediately came to mind was George's special teriyaki sauces.

For many years, George had tinkered with Hawaii-style teriyaki sauces. They were always a big hit with friends, neighbors, family (including those from Hawaii who knew a good teriyaki when they tasted one).

He had never intended for his sauce to be any sort of business venture. He simply liked putting ingredients together and sharing it with others. It truly gave him a sense of his time spent in Maui, growing up under the guidance of his beloved grandmother Lucy Lani.

With an idea now firmly established, Susie retired and they sold off George's lawn care business. They were officially in the teriyaki business although, technically, they didn't have any experience in the food industry beyond being able to make a sauce which their friends and family seemed to enjoy.

Before they could even begin to think about production, George and Susie had to start with an education about the industry. Through the Association of Specialty Food Trade, they were able to take classes to assist them in their endeavor.

They took full advantage of these offerings by taking courses on food production process, distribution margins, health department regulations, city regulations and much more. Once their education was complete, they were able to pursue their new business opportunity.

Through their education, they realized George's approach to his product would have to change. He created his unique sauces "Hawaii-style," meaning he would marry various flavors and taste them. If it tasted good, he would serve it. If it didn't, he would add a sprinkle of this, or a dash of that, and taste it again.

Delivering a product for consumers meant he needed to clearly define a recipe for not only legal/packaging purposes, but also to ensure a consistent customer experience with each batch he would produce.

While George is a master of blending Hawaiian flavors, the process of establishing recipes for mass production was a true challenge for him. More so than ever, he was trying to get just the right touch of everything to produce the perfect Hawaii-style teriyaki sauces.

His initial offering was called Pineapple Plum Teriyaki and reminded him of dinners with Grandma Lucy with its sweet aroma and taste. This was a variant of a sauce George always had on hand at home in Reno. At the back of the fridge he had a jar of a similar concoction which was bottomless because he just added to it long before it would ever run out.

With his Pineapple Plum Teriyaki now formalized and bottled with the appropriate label, George and Susie headed to a farmer's market to sell their first batch. Their feedback was positive for the product. People loved the taste and usually picked up a bottle. George and Susie did take note that many mentioned they wanted it to be a little spicier and perhaps even a little less sweet.

Not wanting to miss an opportunity, George went back to work to create a second flavor line. He created Spicy Garlic Teriyaki, which would soon be outpacing the Pineapple Plum version and become their bestseller, which is the position it still holds today.

After conquering the farmer's market scene, George and Susie felt confident their product was ready for the supermarket shelves. At this same time, Whole Foods® was just coming to Reno. With a reputation for supporting local businesses, they approached buyers there. Mr. G's Hawaii-Style Teriyaki was accepted to Whole Foods®, and George and Susie were pleasantly surprised with the ease in which it was to work with such a large company.

Knowing that getting on the shelves doesn't ensure lasting placement, George and Susie went to work offering in-store demonstrations. Just like at the farmer's markets, customers loved the inspired tastes of George's blends. Soon, Mr. G's Hawaii-Style Teriyaki was rotating through the stores enough to garner the attention of management at Whole Foods®. Appearing on their sales target reports meant Mr. G's had officially carved out a permanent spot on the shelves at Whole Foods®.

This meant they not only expanded distribution within the company, but other supermarkets buyers were also interested in talking to them. Susie notes, "Initially, getting buyers to even talk to you is very challenging. Once you hit the radar on those reports, everyone is willing to talk to you about distribution in their stores."

In addition to customer accolades and expanded distribution, Mr. G's also began to garner the respect of the food industry. Two retirees, who just a short time before had been taking classes to learn about how to sell food, now were rolling in awards. The first contest in which one of their sauces was entered, they won. Gold medal and first place ribbons continued to pile up, including a gold from the prestigious National Barbecue Association for their popular Spicy Garlic Teriyaki.

The next step for George and Susie will be to enlist the assistance of distributors. They have been incredibly successful in taking the company from a start-up to a regional provider. A distributor will take the next large step for them, expanding distribution further-and-further beyond their home base of Reno.

With the success they have experienced in such a short time with just George and Susie doing everything is nothing short of amazing. It is not difficult to envision their brand turning into a nationally recognized name, but it likely won't be George and Susie manning the helm of coast-to-coast distribution.

As retirees already, they are giving the business five more years in which they are going to aggressively grow the company. At that time, they would like to either turn it over to their children, if they are interested, or look for a buyer.

You see, George and Susie both love going to Disney World®. Part of their master plan is to live a snowbird lifestyle. They can enjoy winters in sunny Florida and visit Disney World® as often as they like but still come home to Reno to spend time with friends and family in the summers.

Susie even has a dream beyond that. During those stays in Florida, she plans to work at Disney World®. So, if you find yourself at Disney® in five years, or so, and you happen to be at Splash Mountain™, it very well could be Susie operating the ride for you.

Be sure to tell her what you think of Mr. G's. Don't look for George, though. When they retire again, this time it's for good with him. He's staying home to watch their dogs.

With the success the Kapahees have experienced, it's a no-brainer to state that even in their retirement, whether they are in Reno or Orlando, they will be able to pick up a bottle of Mr. G's at their local grocery store!

Mr. G's Hawaii-Style Teriyaki Photo Album

Mr. G himself, George Kapahee

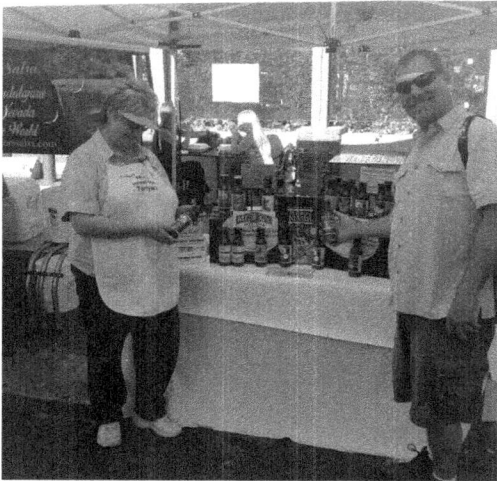

Susie working at a farmer's market

George's grandmother, Lucy Lani

George conducting an in-store demonstration

George's caricature from Mr. G's website versus the real deal…
do you think they captured him with the drawing?

George during researching and development for new flavors

Selecting plums for their original Pineapple Plum Teriyaki

Product lineup

Author's Notes/Resources

The stories of the small companies featured in **Small Brand America** were incredibly fascinating to put together. It seemed like each one was more interesting than the last one as I was interviewing them. My favorite was simply the one I was speaking to at the time since each person was so great in their own way. Whether a small brand had broken through to national distribution, or they were simply fulfilling a need in their hometown, I grew very fond of the individuals who own these companies and their hard work and dedication to the brands they are trying to build.

It's not easy competing on a playing field where you are set-up to fail. The grocery industry caters to, and is fueled by, the large national companies with huge budgets to generate consumer interest and get their items on the shelves. It literally takes millions of dollars to secure shelf space for new product lines for these major companies. Stores automatically want these megabrands over the smaller competitors because they have paid to generate consumer interest via advertising, they pay the stores to promote the product and they pay to get in their warehouses and on their shelves.

As an author, and a consumer, I'm not in any way against the megabrands. For me, though, there is something comforting and even a little fun to think about individuals competing against these giant corporations one consumer at a time.

I do suggest learning more about the companies featured in the book and their products. The more you know about them, and the hard work they are doing to try to get to know you, the more you are likely to try their products. You might just find something you like better than the same brands you've always purchased, simply because "you've always purchased them."

Here's a look at the websites for each:

3 Monkeys Mustard – *3monkeysmustard.com*

Alaskan Brewing Company – *alaskanbeer.com*

Anderson's Maple Syrup – *andersonmaplesyrup.com*

Atlanta Honey Company – *atlantahoneycompany.com*

Berkshire Cheese – *berkshirecheese.com*

Bove's Pasta Sauce – *boves.com*

Brother Bru-Bru's – *brobrubru.com*

CBS Foods, Inc. – *chefbigshake.com*

Des Moines Bacon Company – *desmoinesbaconcompany.com*

Dogtown Pizza – *dogtownpizza.com*

Great Lakes Distillery – *greatlakesdistillery.com*

Hillcrest Ranch Sunol – *hillcrestranch.com*

Hudson Henry Baking Company – hudsonhenrybakingcompany.com

Idaho Candy Company – *idahospud.com*

Jackson Hole Soda Company – *jacksonholesoda.com*

Jimmy's Salad Dressing – *jimmysdressing.com*

Jones Potato Chip Company – *joneschips.com*

Mercer's Dairy – *mercersdairy.com*

Metropolis Coffee – *metropoliscoffee.com*

Mr. G's Hawaii-Style Teriyaki – *mrgsteriyaki.com*

The Nashville Jam Company – *thenashvillejamsco.com*

Portlandia Foods (Portland Ketchup) – *portlandiafoods.com*

Sticky Toffee Pudding Company – *sticktoffeepuddingcompany.com*

Umpqua Oats – *umpquaoats.com*

Verve, Inc. (Glee Gum) – *gleegum.com*

Bonus Section: Recipes

Enjoy these recipes from some of the featured food companies in this publication. For the most part, these recipes have been modified so the listed ingredients are not company-specific. Even so, you are highly encouraged to seek out the products of the companies from **Small Brand America.** If you cannot find them in your local market, most do sell their products via their website. All are listed in the *Author's Notes/Resources* section.

Also, be sure to pick up a copy of **Small Brand America the Cookbook**. These same companies open their vaults to share recipes which either incorporate their product as an ingredient, or serve as complementary dishes. The book contains over 250 recipes. It is available at Amazon in paperback, on Kindle or select local retailers.

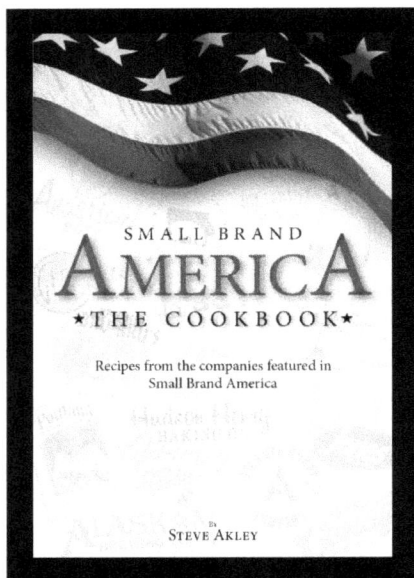

Alaskan Stout Corn Pancakes

Contributor: Alaskan Brewing Company
Reprinted with permission from their book:
Cooking with Alaskan Beer

INGREDIENTS

2	Cups corn meal, coarse ground
2	Cups stout beer
2	Cups all-purpose flour
1	Pint sour cream
2	tbsp. baking powder
½	tbsp. vegetable oil
6	Eggs
1	tsp. salt

DIRECTIONS

- Place cornmeal in a bowl with the beer and allow to soak from several hours to overnight
- Add the remaining ingredients, stirring them into the batter
- Cook pancakes on a hot griddle
- Serve warm with your favorite toppings or cold in place of bread for sandwiches

Bacon Wrapped Beer Bratwurst
Contributor: Des Moines Bacon Company

INGREDIENTS
1   Package precooked beer bratwurst
1   Package hardwood smoked bacon

DIRECTIONS
- Warm deep fryer to 350° F - 375° F
- Start at one end of the bratwurst and apply a slice of bacon using a toothpick to hold it in place
- Continue to wrap the bacon around the bratwurst, using another toothpick to hold it in place at the opposite end
- Drop brats in oil and cook until the bacon is crispy (3 – 5 minutes)
- Work in small batches to keep oil temperature from dropping
- You can serve immediately or set brats on grill or oven to keep warm while you finish cooking

Cheater Chili
Contributor: Dogtown Pizza

INGREDIENTS
1	lb. ground beef
1	Packet Chilio® brand chili seasoning
1	Cup picante salsa, medium
1	Can petite diced tomatoes with green chilis, hot
2	Cans petite diced tomatoes, plain
2	Cans Brooks® Chili Hot Beans

DIRECTIONS
- Brown the ground beef and drain
- Mix all ingredients together
- Bring to a boil and turn low for 45 minutes – 1 hour

Dogtown Pizza owner Rick Schaper notes this chili is perfect for football season and only takes 5 minutes to prepare. He also says you can substitute pulled pork for the ground beef for a unique taste.

Chocolate Cream Spud Pie
Contributor: Idaho Candy Company

INGREDIENTS
8	Idaho Spud Candy Bars
1 ½	Cups of milk
½	Cup heavy whipping cream
1	Pie shell of your choice (pasty or crumb crusts work equally as well)

DIRECTIONS
- Combine candy bars and milk a microwave safe bowl
- Microwave on high, stopping to stir ingredients as they begin to melt
- Continue microwaving until completely melted
- Stir ingredients and let cool as you prepare the next step
- Whip heavy whipping cream with a mixer to give it a fluffy texture
- Save enough whipped cream to decorate top of pie in the bowl and combine the rest into the melted chocolate/milk mixture
- Pour pie into pie shell and refrigerate until it stabilizes
- Add the remainder of whipped heavy cream to the top of the pie

Fettuccini with Berkshire Blue Cheese
Contributor: Berkshire Cheese

INGREDIENTS

1	lb. Fettuccini
1	tsp. shallots, minced
1	tbsp. butter
1	tsp. fresh thyme, minced
1	Cup chicken stock
1	Cup heavy cream
¾	lb. blue cheese
2	tbsp. flour
2	tbsp. roasted walnuts, chopped

DIRECTIONS

- Cook the fettuccini and save for later
- In a pot heat the butter and add the shallots, stir well
- When lightly browned, add thyme and flour, stir well
- Add the chicken stock and cream and mix well to incorporate the flour, stirring well until the sauce thickens
- Lower the heat to simmer and whisk in the cheese, stirring well
- To serve, reheat the noodles and toss with the sauce and garnish with the walnuts

Hawaii-Style Halibut Filets on the Barbecue
Contributor: Mr. G's Hawaii-Style Teriyaki

INGREDIENTS
2	8 oz. halibut filets
6	tbsp. teriyaki sauce
1	tsp. fresh ginger root, grated fine
1	tsp. lemon juice, freshly squeezed/seeds strained out
1	tsp. hot sauce (or to taste if you like it hotter)
1	Red onion, sliced ¼" rings
2	¼" slices of zucchini
1	Whole baby bok choy, washed and cut in ½ lengthwise
8	Sprigs cilantro, washed
2	tbsp. olive oil
2	16" sheets of aluminum foil
	Sea salt and fresh ground pepper

DIRECTIONS
- Brush first aluminum sheet with 1 tbsp. olive oil
- Place filet on oil, brush with 1 tbsp. teriyaki and half of the ginger root, lemon juice and hot sauce
- Salt and pepper to taste
- Layer the filet with half of the red onion, zucchini, baby bok choy and cilantro then drizzles with 2 tbsp. teriyaki
- Bring the two sides of foil together and fold twice to make a sealed pocket around the fish
- Set aside and repeat steps for second piece of fish
- Cook on grill for 8 – 10 minutes until you hear fish boiling for 2 minutes
- Take off of flame and let rest for 5 minutes before opening
- Open pocket carefully as contents are hot/serve with rice

Note: Mr. G's recommends their Pineapple Plum Teriyaki Sauce for this recipe (order some at: mrgsteriyaki.com)

Hot Drunk Shrimp
Contributor: Brother Bru-Bru's

INGREDIENTS
1   Cup silver tequila
1   Cup freshly squeezed citrus juice (suggest: 1 orange, 1 lemon and 1 lime)
¼   Cup fresh peeled ginger, finely minced
2   Cloves garlic, finely minced
1   Jalapeno, seeded and chopped
¼   Cup hot sauce
½   Cup light cooking oil
1   lb. large shrimp, shells on (deveined)
         Wooden skewers

DIRECTIONS
- Combine tequila, juices, garlic, jalapeno and hot sauce in a large bowl
- Slowly whisk in the oil to create an emulsion
- Add the shrimp and allow to marinade for 45 – 60 minutes
- Soak skewers for at least 45 minutes
- Preheat grill on high
- When grill is heated, turn the heat down to medium-high
- Place shrimp on grill and cook until shells are slightly blackened
- While the shrimp are cooking, put the marinade into a small saucepan and heat over medium-high heat until reduced (about 10 minutes)
- Once shrimp is done, transfer skewers to a platter and pour reduced marinade over the top (this could also be used on the side for dipping if preferred)

Serve with yellow saffron rice

Jalapeno Chicken
Contributor: The Nashville Jam Company

INGREDIENTS
- Boneless Chicken Breasts
- Soy sauce
- Jalapeno Jam

DIRECTIONS
- Marinate chicken breast pieces in your favorite soy sauce (minimum of 1 hour/up to overnight)
- Chicken can be stir-fried, baked, broiled or grilled
- During the last few moments of cooking, generously coat each piece with jalapeno jam and allow to glaze

Jolly Rancher Martini
Contributor: Mercer's Dairy

INGREDIENTS

1	2 oz. scoop of Riesling wine ice cream
1	Shot of Midori
1	Shot of Amaretto
1	oz. of sour mix
	Ice

DIRECTIONS

- Add ice cream and liquid ingredients to blender
- Fill blender with ice
- Blend until smooth

Jones' Chip Chicken

Contributor: Jones Potato Chip Company

INGREDIENTS

6	Boneless/skinless chicken breast
6	tbsp. melted butter
1	Large bag (14 oz) of Jones' Original Potato Chips
2	Eggs
¼	Cup milk

Spices:
Fresh ground pepper, garlic powder and smoked paprika

DIRECTIONS

- Preheat oven to 350°
- In a shallow glass dish, whisk together 2 eggs and ¼ cup milk to create a wash for the chicken
- Dip chicken into the egg wash
- *Lightly* sprinkle fresh ground pepper, garlic powder and smoked paprika on top of the chicken breasts
- In a separate bowl, crush up the bag of Jones' Chips
- Dip both sides of the seasoned, egg dipped, chicken in the chip mixture, coating both sides completely
- Lay chicken on open baking sheet that has been lightly sprayed with a non-stick cooking spray
- Drizzle 1 tbsp. of melted butter over the top of each chip-coated piece of chicken
- Baked uncovered for one-hour until the center is cooked

Lasagna
Contributor: Bove's Restaurant

INGREDIENTS
2	Jars marinara or vodka sauce (Bove's recommended)
1/3	lb. thinly sliced mozzarella cheese
¾	1lb. ricotta cheese
½	Grated parmesan cheese
¾	Cup cottage cheese
¾	lb. lasagna noodles (about 24 pieces)
2	tbs. fresh chopped Italian parsley
2	lbs. packages of meatballs (Bove's recommended)
2	tbs. olive oil

DIRECTIONS
- Before starting the lasagna, pour sauce into pot
- Take bags of frozen meatballs and add them to the pot
- Let sit in the refrigerator overnight
- The next day, cook lasagna noodles to the al dente stage in lightly salted water with the olive oil
- Separate the noodles and drain on cotton dish towel
- Preheat oven to 350° F
- Spread a thin layer of sauce from the meatballs to cover bottom of pan
- Cover with noodles and then a layer of the three cheeses
- Add meatballs by crumbling on top of the layer
- Continue to build layers by repeating the steps
- When the process is complete, add a layer of sauce, dust with mozzarella, parmesan cheese and parsley
- Bake 30 – 40 minutes, until bubbly and light brown around the edges
- Let stand 5 – 10 minutes before cutting and serving

*This is the same recipe that was featured on the Food Network Show **Throwdown with Bobby Flay** and NBC's **Today Show***

Milwaukee Spa Treatment
Contributor: Great Lakes Distillery

INGREDIENTS

3	Cucumber slices
2	Small cubes of honeydew melon
1	Small stalk of lemon grass
½	oz. premium gin
2 ½	oz. premium vodka
	Kosher salt

DIRECTIONS

- Muddle 2 cucumber slices, honeydew, lemon grass, a pinch of kosher salt and the gin at the bottom of a mixing glass
- Add vodka and fill shaker with ice
- Shake well and double strain into a chilled cocktail glass
- Garnish with a cucumber wheel and sprinkle with kosher salt

Parmesan Tilapia
Contributor: Jimmy's Salad Dressing & Dips

INGREDIENTS

½	Cup parmesan cheese, shredded	2	tbsp. fresh lemon juice
		¼	tsp. black pepper
1/8	Cup butter, softened	2	lb. tilapia filets
3	tbsp. tartar sauce		

DIRECTIONS

- Preheat broiler on high
- Use cooking spray to coat broiler pan
- In a small bowl, mix together parmesan, butter, tartar sauce, lemon juice and pepper and set aside
- Arrange tilapia filets in a single layer on the broiling pan
- Broil for 2 – 3 minutes
- Flip the filet and broil 2 more minutes
- Remove the filets from the oven and cover them with parmesan/tartar sauce mixture
- Broil for 2 more minutes or until the topping and browned and the fish flakes easily with a fork (use caution not to overcook)

Sunol Sundae
Contributor: Hillcrest Ranch

INGREDIENTS
- Vanilla ice cream
- Extra virgin olive oil
- Sea salt

DIRECTIONS
- Drizzle extra virgin olive oil over a scoop of vanilla ice cream
- Sprinkle with sea salt

Tangy Maple Meatballs

Contributor: Anderson's Maple Syrup, Inc.

INGREDIENTS

Meatballs

½	lb. ground beef	1	Egg
½	lb. ground pork	¼	Cup chopped onion
2	tbsp. dried parsley flakes	½	tsp. salt
1	tsp. Worcestershire sauce	1/8	tsp. pepper

Sauce

1	tbsp. cornstarch	1	tbsp. vinegar
1	tsp. dry mustard	½	Cup pure maple syrup
¼	tsp. salt	¼	Cup water

DIRECTIONS

- Preheat oven to 350°
- Combine ground meats, onion, egg, parsley, Worcestershire sauce, salt and pepper
- Form into 1 ½ inch balls
- Place in an 8" square pan and bake for 20 minutes
- While baking, combine cornstarch, dry mustard and salt in a small saucepan
- Gradually stir in vinegar, pure maple syrup and water
- Cook over a medium heat stirring frequently until thickened and bubbly
- Drain fat from meatballs
- Pour sauce over meatballs
- Return to 350° oven to cook 20-minutes longer

Serves four

Yummy Meatloaf
Contributor: Atlanta Honey Company

INGREDIENTS
½   lb. ground pork
1 ½   lbs. ground beef
2   Eggs, beaten
1   Cup cracker crumbs
1 ½   tsp. salt
½   tsp. milk
2   tbsp. honey
½   Cup ketchup

DIRECTIONS
- Preheat oven to 375° F
- Combine all ingredients except ketchup and mix well
- Shape into a loaf 2 ½" thick and place into a greased pan
- Cover top of loaf with ketchup
- Bake for one hour or until thoroughly cooked
- Optional: spread with more ketchup before serving

Bibliography/Sources

In addition to the websites of the companies profiled (all listed in the **Author's Notes/Resources** *section), the following resources were also utilized to create this book:*

American Dialect Society Website: *americandialect.org* (Word of the Year research)

BrainyQuote® website: *brainyquote.com* (W. Disney & M. Field quotes)

Brewer's Association website: *brewersassociation.org* (brewer stats)

Bruce Langhorne's website: *brucelanghorne.com*

Electronic Documents: *History of Andersons, Anderson History* and *Norman Anderson Hall of Fame*, Steven Anderson.

Interview with 3 Monkeys Mustard Owner Dan Collins: July 26, 2013.

Interview with Alaskan Brewing Company Marketing Specialist Luke Bauer: July 23, 2013.

Interview with Anderson's Maple Syrup, Inc. President/Owner Steve Anderson: July 11, 2013.

Interview with Atlanta Honey Company Owner Grant Giddens: July 23, 2013.

Interview with Berkshire Cheese Cheesemaker Ira Grable: August 6, 2013.

Interview with Bove's Restaurant Owner Mark Bove: July 26, 2013.

Interview with Brother Bru-Bru's Owner Cynthia Riddle: July 24, 2013.

Interview with CBS Foods, Inc. President Shawn Davis: August 16, 2013.

Interview with Des Moines Bacon Company Owner Jim Reis: July 10, 2013.

Interview with Dogtown Pizza Owner/Operators Meredith Schaper and Rick Schaper: July 26, 2013.

Interview with Great Lakes Distillery Owner Guy Rehorst: August 17, 2013.

Interview with Hillcrest Farms Sunol Owner Kathleen D. Elliott: July, 19, 2013.

Interview with Hudson Henry Baking Company Founder Hope Lawrence: July 26, 2013

Interview with Idaho Candy Company "Candyman" David Wagers: June 26, 2013.

Interview with Jackson Hole Soda Company President Bill Leary: August 8, 2013.

Interview with Jimmy's Salad Dressing and Dips Owner Tom Slightam: July 24, 2013.

Interview with Jones Potato Chip Company, Owner and President Bob Jones: June 28, 2013.

Interview with Mercer's Dairy Chief Operating Officer Dalton Givens and Owner Roxaina Hurlburt: July 19, 2013.

Interview with Metropolis Coffee Company Communications and Social Media Manager Seth J. Alexander: July 30, 2013.

Interview with Mr. G's Hawaii-Style Teriyaki Owner Susie Kapahee: August 7, 2013.

Interview with The Nashville Jam Company Owner Cortney Baron: July 28, 2013.

Interview with The Nashville Jam Company Co-Founder Gary Baron: July 3, 2013.

Interview with Portlandia Foods Owner Jeff Bergadine: July 22, 2013.

Interview with Sticky Toffee Pudding Company Founder Tracy Claros: July 26, 2013.

Interview with Umpqua Oats Owner Sheri Price: August 1, 2013.

Interview with Verve, Inc. Founder & CEO Deborah Schimberg: August 1, 2013.

Photographs

All photographs, in the sections of each business featured, have been utilized with permission from the respective companies with the following four exceptions:

Mercer's Dairy soft serve cone (p. 119) – Brandy Szewcyzyk

Girl with birds on Portland Ketchup label (p. 140) – Steve Akley

Jackson Hole, Wyoming Sign (p. 240) – Steve Akley

Welcome to Colorado sign (p. 240) – Steve Akley

Special Thanks

To my mom, Sandy Akley, for her help in editing this book.

Thanks to my wife Amy and to my daughter Cat for just being themselves.

Hats off to Mark Hansen (*mappersmark@gmail.com*) for the great cover design. He's the greatest graphic artist you will ever find!

The following individuals from the featured companies not only couldn't have been nicer, without their help this book would not have been possible:

Seth Alexander, Metropolis Coffee Company

Steven Anderson, Anderson's Pure Maple Syrup

Cortney & Gary Baron, The Nashville Jam Company

Luke Bauer, Alaskan Brewing Company

Jeff Bergadine, Portlandia Foods

Mark Bove, Bove's Restaurant

Tracy Claros, Sticky Toffee Pudding Company

Dan Collins, 3 Monkeys Mustard

Shawn Davis, CBS Foods, Inc.

Kathleen Elliott, Hillcrest Ranch Sunol

Grant Giddens, Atlanta Honey Company

Dalton Givens, Mercer's Dairy

Ira Grable, Berkshire Cheese, LLC

Roxaina Hurlburt – Mercer's Dairy

Bob Jones, Jones Potato Chip Company's

Susie Kapahee, Mr. G's Hawaii-Style Teriyaki

Geoff & Marcy Larson, Alaskan Brewing Company

Hope Lawrence, Hudson Henry Baking Company

Bill Leary, Jackson Hole Soda Company

Molly Lederer, Verve, Inc.

Sheri Price, Umpqua Oats

Guy Rehorst, Great Lakes Distillery

Jim Reis, Des Moines Bacon Company

Cynthia Riddle, Brother Bru-Bru's Hot Sauce Company

Meredith & Rick Schaper, Dogtown Pizza Company

Deborah Schimberg, Verve, Inc.

Tom Slightam, Jimmy's Salad Dressing

David Wagers, Idaho Candy Company

Lastly, lots of love for my father, Larry Akley. He's always with us in spirit.

In Loving Memory of Larry Akley
1942 – 2012

Dad's badge photo compliments of Kelly Brooks (thanks sis!)

Meet Team Akley

It takes more than just an author to publish a book. Here's a look at the team that supports my efforts:

Sandy Akley/Mom
Responsibilities: Book editing, guerilla marketing, conventional marketing, grassroots marketing, local p.r. and team cheerleader

Amy Akley/Wife
Responsibilities: Mailroom, guerilla marketing and taxes

Cat Akley/Daughter
Responsibilities: Social media and guerilla marketing

Kelly Brooks/Sister, Nathan Brooks/Nephew, Mason Brooks/Nephew, Pierce Lojkovic/Nephew, Greyson Lojkovic/Nephew, Tessa Sciuto/Niece, Debbie Zebas/Aunt, Lee Ann Sciuto/Sister-in-Law
Responsibilities: Guerilla marketing

Larry Akley/Father
Responsibility: Inspiration

About the Author

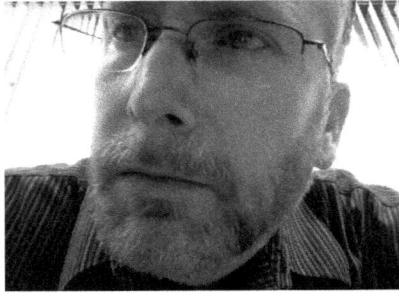

Steve Akley is a lifelong St. Louis resident. He lives with his wife Amy, their daughter Cat and a 22 lb. Maine Coon cat named Leo.

The family enjoys travel, Christmas music, watching NFL® football and spending weekends at their second home: a log cabin in a lake community about an hour south of their home. Steve reports that the entire family shares his fondness for small brands trying to make it in the United States… and ice cream.

Steve's other interests include: bourbon, Starbucks®, the art of SHAG,the Red Hot Chili Peppers, blueberries, huckleberries, growing chili peppers, the music of Dick Dale (*dickdale.com*), chicken wings, turtles/tortoises, hawks, banana slugs, Abraham Lincoln (same birthday as Steve), Harry Truman (Missouri's only president), everything St. Louis, Hawaii, New Mexico, Florida, Maine (best blueberries), poker/card games, Seinfeld, Quentin Tarantino movies, metal advertising signs and bacon.

Small Brand America is his fourth published work, but he has lots of other great book ideas. Sign up for his newsletter, or check out his latest work, on his website: *steveakley.com.*

Steve also maintains an author's page on *Amazon.com.* Just search his name on the site.

Steve can be reached via email: *info@steveakley.com*

Find Steve on Social Media

@steveakley

Follow Steve to see what he's up to!

WORDPRESS

http://steveakley.wordpress.com

Steve posts weekly updates about his writing projects on his blog. You can sign up to have his weekly posts emailed to you!

Steve Akley

Like Steve's page on Facebook

Also by Steve Akley

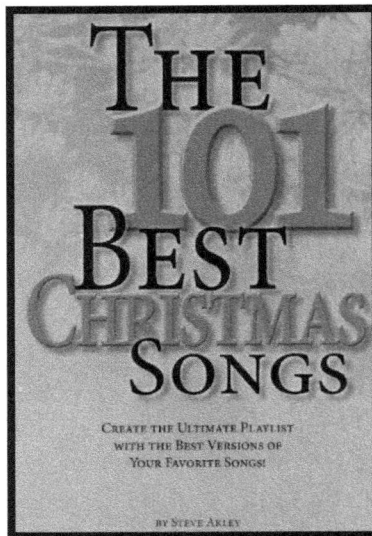

Christmas is the best time of the year, why settle for anything less than the best holiday music? *The 101 Best Christmas Songs* is designed to assist you in creating the ultimate playlist by focusing on the best versions of Christmas favorites.

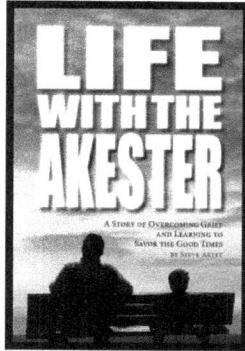

Life with the Akester takes you through the journey of a son when he loses his beloved father (Larry "Akester" Akley) very unexpectedly to a heart attack. Author Steve Akley takes us through the darkest emotions following this family tragedy and how he begins the healing process of grief in an unexpected way.

The book is broken into two distinct parts. The first part walks the reader through the process Steve went through told via first-person narrative. The reader sees the perspective of Steve who begins to establish his "new normal," as he states, via a series of happenstance events in his life.

The second part of the book Steve savors the good times with his father by sharing some of the truly funny moments from his life. It was an ongoing family source of non-stop laughs to reiterate the unbelievable capers Steve's father got himself in. Whether it was bathroom humor, public humiliation or a completely head-scratching decision, the Akester always kept his family and friends in stitches with his hijinks. Prepare yourself to laugh out loud as you read the unique moments only the Akester could have gotten himself into!

The end result is a loving tribute to a father by a son who can't have another moment with his father, but can relish his life by sharing his story.

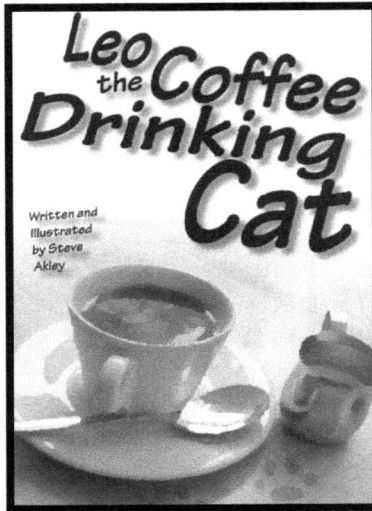

Leo the Coffee Drinking Cat is a children's book that highlights the special bond between Leo, a talking/coffee-drinking cat and his 3 year-old owner, Catherine. When Leo tells her he dreams of visiting the coffee paradise of Starbucks, it's up to Catherine to get him there.

COMING SOON:
SMALL BRAND AMERICA II

Steve's Website

Steve's website is the hub for information about his work, where to find his books and a means to reach out to him. Through his website, he has a sign-up to receive his newsletter which he publishes four times a year (March 1, June 1, September 1 and December 1). To learn more about his books, and to sign-up for his newsletter, check out:

www.steveakley.com

www.ingramcontent.com/pod-product-compliance
Lightning Source LLC
Chambersburg PA
CBHW060543200326
41521CB00007B/462